ANCHORING POINTS FOR CORPORATE DIRECTORS

ANCHORING POINTS FOR CORPORATE DIRECTORS

Obeying the Unenforceable

Robert K. Mueller

Q

QUORUM BOOKS
Westport, Connecticut • London

Library of Congress Cataloging-in-Publication Data

Mueller, Robert Kirk.
    Anchoring points for corporate directors : obeying the
unenforceable / Robert K. Mueller.
      p.   cm.
    Includes bibliographical references and index.
    ISBN 1–56720–068–0 (alk. paper)
    1. Directors of corporations.   2. Chief executive officers.
   3. Corporate governance.   I. Title.
HD2745.M788   1996
658.4'22—dc20   96–2214

British Library Cataloguing in Publication Data is available.

Library of Congress Catalog Card Number: 96–2214
ISBN: 1–56720–068–0

First published in 1996

Quorum Books, 88 Post Road West, Westport, CT 06881
An imprint of Greenwood Publishing Group, Inc.

Printed in the United States of America

The paper used in this book complies with the
Permanent Paper Standard issued by the National
Information Standards Organization (Z39.48–1984).

10   9   8   7   6   5   4   3   2   1

Contents

Preface

One of history's most remarkable organizational achievements is the publicly owned enterprise governed by an independent board of trustees or directors. It has served society well for most of this century in the West. It is an unrivaled creator of wealth, employment, social services, and benefits. However, unless actions are taken to improve the conduct of publicly held corporations, this organizational form may become an endangered species.

The key issue is board effectiveness, causing enterprise governance to be put on trial in both the for-profit and not-for-profit domains. Sagas of the United Way, Empire Blue Cross–Blue Shield, or the General Motors, IBM, American Express, Metallgesellschaft, Maxwell Communication, BCCI, and other headline boardroom stories concern the very foundation and principles on which any strong enterprise should be built, and the underlying issues faced in an incorporated Western enterprise, large or small.

An understanding of just one, but important, issue to be faced is this: The practice and reality that the chairman, chief executive officer (CEO), managing director, or executive director who does not take advantage of the board of directors as his or her most important asset, greatest strength, and conscience, is a leader who does not understand the potential power of the partnership between the board of directors and the executive leader.

There are many other important understandings, concepts, and touchstones of thought which exist in the covenantal relationships between directors. These are employed intuitively by directors in their self-educating and exploratory problem-solving (heuristic) techniques in efforts to improve enterprise performance. One of these heuristics is the adjustment from an anchor. The process used is referred to as *anchoring* (thinking about a problem from different starting points or anchors).[1]

The endangered species—the status quo organization that does not change—is not confined to large, publicly held corporations. When looking at the United States, it is important to recognize the size and scope of what is called the "parallel economy," wherein the family or closely held business universe approaches and possibly exceeds the size of the publicly owned universe. The relative share of family businesses among all businesses is surprisingly high, ranging, for example, between 61 percent in France and 82 percent in Germany, 83 percent in Austria, and all countries averaging 66 percent.[2]

In the United States, a conservative estimate of closely held family businesses generates $1.5 trillion of the gross national product (GNP) annually. Including distribution, these businesses number between 1.7 and 12.9 million entities. Excluding sole proprietorships, small family businesses number about 1.7 million. This compares to over 54,000 publicly traded companies on the various stock exchanges. Therefore, family businesses outnumber publicly owned businesses by more than fifty to one. The family business universe approaches and possibly exceeds the publicly owned universe (a parallel economy).[3]

Considering all U.S. corporations with their directors for these enterprises, it is estimated that 400,000 to 500,000 directors are in the cohort of such demographics. To expect that all of these directors have to be perfect is idealistic and certainly not feasible. Performance and behavior of directors are guided by various laws, statutes, regulations, values, attitudes, beliefs, customs, myths, and norms. These explicit canons are the subject of most writings about board directorship.

A recent contribution toward better board operation is a book based on the wealth of experience of William G. Bowen, currently president of the Andrew W. Mellon Foundation, former president of Princeton University, and a board member of Merck, *Reader's Digest*, the Rockefeller Group, Denison University, the Public Broadcasting Laboratory of National Education Television, the Sloan Foundation, the Smithsonian, and more.

Bowen's book, *Inside the Boardroom: Governance by Directors and Trustees* (New York: John Wiley & Sons, 1994) develops and discusses some "20 presumptive norms" by which boards of directors and trustees might operate well. Based on his broad personal experience, these notions are his judgment on how enterprises ought to function as a rule. He underscores the word "presumptive" because the norms should always be challenged, and there are good reasons not to function that way in a given setting. Bowen states, "I don't believe in formula-driven solutions at all, but I do believe in having a starting point to use in organizing one's thinking."

The presumptive norms provide a prescriptive modality for curing board ills. Topics covered include board size and turnover; director term limits, competence, diversity and independence; avoiding conflicts of interest; former CEO's continuing board service; director and trustee compensation; the double-C controversy (combined CEO–chairman); committee roles; meeting frequency and agenda management; outside professional advisors; CEO selection and succession planning; and board information systems.

This model for board operations nails down key norms encountered by an experienced director, trustee, and executive leader. It will help, as Bowen says, in "having a starting point to use in organizing one's thinking."

Thinking constructively about governance conduct also requires thinking about individual director or trustee value systems, beliefs, and attitudes. An essential challenge beyond how the board should operate is that of the unenforceable elements of conduct of individual directors (and of boards as a group). These also are the most interesting. They are vexatious, and they are the focus of anchoring points.

With the benefit of personal experiences, plus references in previous writings, a reprise is included of imperfect experiences from my own and others' boardroom exposures. If understood better, such anchors would have helped my past performance as a director these many years.

Anchoring points are offered herein by one imperfect director to others, including those yearning for his or her first board seat. These anchors concern the concept of servanthood without dominance in the boardroom. In particular, they are about obeying the unenforceable while navigating the shining seas of corporate governance in the 1990s and beyond.

Moulton's Manners

During World War I, Lord John Fletcher Moulton, a high official in the British Munitions industry, articulated the "three great domains of human action." This was in a speech, entitled "Law and Manners," presented at the Authors Club, London, in 1914.

The first domain is the domain of "positive law," where law in all of its various forms properly binds and constrains us. The second is the domain of "free choice" or "absolute freedom," where citizens can properly claim complete freedom of personal action. The third is the domain of "manners" or "obedience to the unenforceable." According to Moulton, this is the sphere where we do what we should do, though not obliged to do so by any law. It is an area where neither law nor free choice controls. Moulton believed that a nation's greatness, its civilization, rests in the extent of this third domain.

Many boards of directors are content to confine their activities, if possible, to the first domain of positive law. The free choice domain requires some individual director initiative—a rare trait these days with the liabilities and complexities involved in being an effective director.

The third and normative domain of Moulton's obedience to the unenforceable implies, first, that there exists an initiative—a will—in a boardroom context, and, second, that the chairman, CEO, the directors (both independent outsiders and executive insiders) obey their instincts in surfacing the core issues before the meeting if such issues can be identified.

The problem, of course, comes in the obedience to the intuitive and responsible concerns for board effectiveness when others do not share such concerns, or have common value systems, ethics, ideologies, or attitudes and instincts. Trade-offs involve risking the rupture of relationships with the shareowners, the chairman, other independent directors, or the chief executive. This is particularly so if none of these persons shares the same apprehension or concern over board matters not on the agenda because of positive law requirements or even free choice of the agenda maker.

Directors can be great if they respect this domain of good corporate practice. This is shaped by personal conscience, values, morals, beliefs, attitudes, aspirations, vision, and the corporate culture. In other words, when you are in the board seat, you are on your own.

HAZLITT'S HYPOTHESIS

Over five generations ago, English critic and essayist William Hazlitt aptly hypothesized, "Elegance is necessary to the fine gentleman, dignity is proper to noblemen, and majesty to kings." Today, he would have added, "Conduct becoming a fiduciary."[1]

In his time, this British essayist career-hopped with style, vigor, rhythm, and contemptuousness. Thus, he has some basis for his pronunciamento. After abandoning theology and renouncing painting, he applied his metaphysical acumen to a wide range of topics in politics, theater, and art, where gentlemen, noblemen, and royalty frequented.

Elegance for fine gentlemen applied also to nineteenth-century top managers and directors. Qualifications for such positions in society demanded fine manners, bearing, and behavior appropriate for those elegant times. We still have a few such nineteenth-century minded directors today. However, the twenty-first-century director will certainly have to possess more than elegance in manners. Elegance in both managerial ability and directorship is required. Elegance in the boardroom not only implies refinement and experience but independence, professionalism, intuition, integrity, effective communications, and some rational precision.

Hazlitt's 1825 essay, "Spirit of the Age," was considered his best by many. It may offer an appropriate creed for the new spirit of elegance needed to cope with increasing dysfunctional behavior in many corporations, both at the board and the executive management level. In part, this behavior is a benign attitude toward a regrettable deflection of human resources. The deflection is caused by conflicts between individual and institutional careers. This discordant phenomenon pervades some boards of directors, including those where the leadership clings to the obsolete concept of a board dominated by the chairman and/or CEO.

The notion of a board free from domination by inside directors, the CEO or the chairman, with informed and qualified independent directors acting in an independent, unaffiliated, disinterested manner, is a concept high on the corporate governance agenda. This notion is being extended to observing not only the laws, norms, statutes, and regulations, but also those matters which concern the unenforceable or covenantal side of relationships between the individual director and the corporation board itself.

The current condition, which I consider to be directorship's inelegant dysfunction, is this book's target message. Certain anchoring points for judgment and knowledge are suggested herein. These are an effort to improve the effectiveness and performance of both individual directors and the board as a group. Boards of directors are prime movers in history's most remarkable organizational achievement—the public enterprise governed by an independent coalition of willing fiduciaries. Directors and boards must consciously engage in an organizational learning process of obeying the unenforceable.

Caveat Lector
(and Would-Be Director)

Managers manage, directors govern, and shareholders own the corporation. I have authored nine books on corporate governance—that body of lore dealing with how members of boards of directors should behave and what they are supposed to accomplish. But this book is largely concerned with what really goes on in that corporate crypt known as the boardroom. It begins with a cautionary note and goes on to give some touchstones and advice about survival in the corporate briarpatch of governance, despite imperfect directorship.

If you think about the rewards that may come with a seat on a board of, say, a publicly owned corporation, or even a private one of modest dimensions, consider the following first:

- In 1978, more total years of prison time were assessed against corporate officials, including directors, under the Sherman & Clayton antitrust statutes than during the preceding eighty-nine years of the act's existence. Since then, winds of change continue to howl at the boardroom doors. The director scandals of the nineties are being encountered worldwide.

- Corporate gadflies, legal and government advisers, institutional investors, academic analysts, and journalists are attacking director performance. They fail to stress the covenantal side, the potential and means for improving director service, and the help of anchoring points for education and judgment.

- Problems of board accountability, inactivity, abuse of power, and dereliction of duty are more than can be dealt with by public opinion or by regulatory or legal reform. To reach an understanding of human frailty, corrective action must come from directors themselves obeying the unenforceable as set forth in Moulton's Manners.

Yes, there is trouble in ample measure at the very top. Surprisingly, there is no shortage of volunteers, even though the path to the boardroom may be a great deal more difficult than aspirants can imagine.[1]

My First Directorship . . . Rx for Failure. This took place in a start-up enterprise with its boardroom without walls or an understanding of the role of a board of directors. The fiduciary status was achieved through the simple device of three close friends forming a corporation, Line and Staff Inc. (L&S), Springfield, Massachusetts. The three of us worked full-time for the same employer, a plastics company in nearby Indian Orchard. We had only our personal time, reputations, and a small investment at risk in this moonlighting private venture.

We were energetic in those days, seeking relaxation from pothering company pressures. We covertly started this Junior Achievement-sized enterprise outside of work hours. The incorporation involved a small investment from each of us, and we became the corporation's founder directors. The board included two founders' wives to add some style and artistic talent to the enterprise. This was a model, privately owned venture but with no outside advisers, investors, or directors.

Since the first role of a director is to legitimatize a corporation—all corporations must have directors—three of us ("Bud" Harrison Lyman, an attorney; Ralph Hansen, a marketing executive and inventor; and I) registered L&S in 1958 and elected ourselves and the two spouses directors. This smallish enterprise was to create, manufacture, and market clever self-help aids for business—studio-card printed communications, novelty items poking fun at the executive suite, and a problem-solving service for harassed businessmen and women.

As chairman and CEO, I saw that our board meetings paralleled those of typical closely held corporations. Boardroom mates were close friends, and we convened only because the law says you have to have a directorate. Bud wrote the minutes before each recorded board meeting in order to keep our legal and tax skirts clean. We never really had a formal board meeting but fulfilled and recorded these statutory requirements in combination with our management meetings.

Before relating what we learned from this modest, entrepreneurial, three-family business venture, it is best to tell some of the experiences we weathered in three years of this ambitious, sandbox-sized, corporate experiment.

In retrospect, the product line was ingenuous, somewhat cutesy, but had a gloss of novelty. I find almost twoscore years later that the pathology of executive management and director patterns of behavior is, of course, the same. People—even business executives—seldom change their motivation and emotional traits. Their hidden agendas, their ethics, value systems, career objectives, peer relationships, search for self-esteem, and self-actualization remain generic.

L&S's business focus played on what we then perceived as esteem needs of executives. They were expected to respond to our company's unique line of products and services advertised in business media and by direct mail.

L&S's sparkplug and expert in marketing, promotion, and idea creation was Ralph Hansen, now deceased. In his regular job, he was market research and development director. He had racked up some original product and promotional schemes, notably Astroturf for sports arenas. This was a new application for synthetic fibers. Ralph's creative talents became riotous with L&S. Bud's legal conservatism and my engineering bent subdued, to a degree, some of the far-out products and services we discussed in our board-cum-management strategy sessions. Our lady directors helped, too, in toning down the more sappy product creations. To give a flavor of our business, I include a few survivor projects we launched in the short life of L&S. They are the following:

- *The International T.I.E. Club.* This was a membership club founded in 1960 with the creed, "Take It Easy," for burnt-out, overworked executives. Membership cards were available for those who agreed to follow the dicta and high purpose of the Ten Important Edicts for which the Club was founded. These edicts concerned platitudinous health hints, admonition to spend time with family, restriction of working hours, and the like. In addition, identification accessories were for sale including a monogrammed T.I.E. tie, a T.I.E. buckled belt, and T.I.E. cuff links. One of the first of many rude awakenings we received was an anonymous letter the week after we advertised the Club and its accessories in the *New Yorker*. The envelope enclosed a clipping from the *New York Times* offering similar monogrammed ties and belts at 40 percent less than our advertisement. We were blighted.

- *Self-Appraisal Guide for Salesmen*. A recently proven guide developed by L&S to improve your sales organization.

- *Package Evaluation Chart*. A neat and quick device for measuring the value of the packaging used for consumer products (an L&S created executive aid, also now available on a request basis).

- *L&S Low-Cost Armchair Consulting Service in Certain Management and Administration Fields*. Available only after a preliminary casing of your problem by correspondence, a free estimate of the service we can offer you.

- *Studio Card Communicators*. These were built around graffiti-type one-liners, topical for the late 1950s. They are embarrassingly adolescent for the 1990s business sophisticate, evident from the following:

  —Isn't there some way we can settle our dispute without resorting to agreement?

  —Reach a media man—advertise on swizzle sticks!

  —Money is the root of all evil, and man needs roots.

  —Bo Peep did it for the insurance.

  —Somebody has to bury the undertakers.

  —Managing is like drinking out of a fire hose.

This reprise of L&S's product line explains, in part, why the company went down the tubes. Looking at the experience in a kindly way, we were not young enough to know everything, so our enterprise flamed out in three years as competition reacted and sales plummeted. Collapse was triggered when two of the directors were relocated geographically.

The lessons we learned were these: (1) never do anything for the first time; (2) at some time in the life cycle of virtually every corporation, its ability to succeed in spite of the board and management runs out; (3) never undertake a business venture without some independent advice, either on the board or in an advisory role; and (4) there are more buzzards than carcasses.

Supplementing these lessons are unenforceable tenets common to many publicly held and closely held enterprises. They are the following:

- Three crises normally occur with the owners of a closely held corporation. They are (1) the crisis of succession, the dynastic tendency; (2) the crisis of reorganization with generational or management change; and (3) the crisis of letting go when owners of their descendants are in no position to run the firm. L&S never got far enough off the launch pad to have even the first crisis!

- Having a product line doesn't mean you have a business. Market research revealing demands, needs, and customers is vital. L&S had none of this and was ambition- rather than condition-driven.

- It is difficult to see the business picture when you're inside the frame. L&S had no outside directors or advisers. We failed to be realistic about our customer prospects.

- Harvard Business School Professor Theodore Levitt's baby robin theory of education prevailed, with our marketing expert, Ralph, acting as the teacher. Newly hatched birds (Bud and I) thrived from the mother robin's assorted gatherings (for products and services) stuffed down their eagerly opened gullets. The students are supposed to listen and learn the professional *hochsprache* similarly stuffed. It is presumed that what's said is relevant, what's relevant is heard, what's heard is understood, what's understood is retained, and what's retained is usable and used. L&S's problem was lack of experience of the founders, no outsider perspective, and gullibility of all three of us to realities of the marketplace.

- Venture capitalists would call the L&S demise an incompetent failure. A competent failure is sophisticated talk referring to the notion in a value system that to fail because of incompetence is intolerable. Failure after a competent effort is excusable and understandable.

- "Mouse milking" was the 1980 phrase used to imply undue effort expended to accomplish a small result. In L&S's case, the result was a three-year life span before external career moves gracefully separated the three founders geographically.

L&S was folded quietly with minimum dishonor by advising the Corporation's Division, Secretary of the Commonwealth of Massachusetts, in order to be legal and avoid costs of further filing fees. The small stigmata that each of us wore for only a short time thereafter was rationalized as a business battle scar in a battleground for which we were unprepared.

Since we had no real customer or financial obligations, our disappearance from the global business scene was a nonevent. The experience was, in retrospect, worth the effort. The learnings proved to be useful later in our respective chosen careers. Entrepreneurial directors don't have to be perfect. But they had better have access to independent, disinterested, unaffiliated, informed outside advisers.

ANCHORING POINTS FOR CORPORATE DIRECTORS

1

Groupthink Pathology:
How to Avoid This

Groupthink is a peccable problem. Its main theme is concurrence seeking. This pathological condition introduces a risk bias that is found in all decision-making groups, namely, in an entrepreneurial enterprise, partnerships, a closely or publicly owned company, churches, schools, hospitals, governments, associations, cooperatives, fraternities, or activist groups. While family firms are not unique, kinship bonding may encourage groupthink tendencies.

When successful, groupthink can be a significant force. However, the concept of groupthink pinpoints an entirely different source of potential trouble, residing neither in the individuals nor the organizational setting. The anchoring point is the board of directors.

Over and beyond all the familiar sources of human error is a powerful source of defective judgment that arises in any cohesive group such as a board of directors. Scholars have found that, in group dynamics, there is a concurrence-seeking tendency fostering over-optimism, an illusion of invulnerability, stereotypical views, the practice of self-censorship, lack of vigilance, and, in the case of some in-groups, sloganistic thinking about the weakness and immorality of out-groups. The Bay of Pigs invasion, the decision to launch the Challenger, and the remarkable march of democracy in Eastern Europe are examples of the impact of groupthink on a broad scale.

Individuals within any group can become emotionally committed to group decisions. As a result, their own personal attitudes and models of reality shift to that of the group in an attempt to maintain inner consistency. The result is the group's inability to change a failing policy.

Some boards of directors even develop what are called mindguards. For example, self-appointed members of the board, family, or company staff try to shield the directors from information that may go against shared beliefs. This practice is not new. Egyptian viziers, physicians, and magicians had established roles of adhering to the enshrined wisdom of ancient sacrosanct writings. This was so unchallengeable that they often stagnated progress, shielding the pharaoh from changes and advances in fundamental knowledge and experience.

A CASE OF GENERATIONAL GROUPTHINK

Five years ago, groupthink gripped the board and top executives of a Missouri-based manufacturer of plastic parts for industrial uses, for example, auto parts, appliances, electrical components. The company, in its third generation of family ownership and management, retained the founder's reputation for superior quality and service in the Midwest and had entered the export market. Extended-family ownership and management included four board seats out of seven. The three outside directors were the family attorney, family banker, and an in-law . . . peccable persons due to their potential conflicts of interests.

Military demand for the products had been the major driving force since the beginning. The entire family group consistently rationalized early warnings and other disturbing data indicating a reduction in government requirements for their products, despite the declining backlog. The three outside directors were also entrained in the company's historical dedication to government business. No reevaluation of strategy and policy or evaluation of alternatives was forthcoming. The board assumed no devil's advocate role in its decision making when considering the executive management's recommendations.

As a longtime plastics industry colleague, I was asked by the chairman–chief executive officer (CEO) to advise the board. The task was difficult since their hands-on type of operation and management culture were incompatible with modern strategic planning concepts.

In fact, the CEO boasted to me of the absence of a long-range plan and a planning staff. After separate working sessions with the three key family members of the board and management, it was possible to get the CEO to accept the need for a formal planning function and development of alternative future plans. The obvious objective was to decrease dependence on government business. Revectoring of the company would take two years of monitoring. At last checkup, dependence on government contracts was down to less than 30 percent of annual sales.

CHANGE AND GROUPTHINK IN THE YPO

Every corporation goes through topside changes and faces groupthink. Even the most effective managers come and go. Change and groupthink are priority matters on the agenda of the Young President's Organization (YPO), an international group consisting of executives who have become president before age forty and who are shipped out of the group as old-timers when they turn fifty.

When I was a member of the Boston chapter, presidents from all sorts of businesses—retail, finance, marketing, hotel management, manufacturing—would have the same sort of awakening to the rules of the game. While each one had his own set of problems with his own set of owners, I found two difficulties that were common denominators: Each president had inherited some sort of transfer-of-power problem upon assuming his new position. Owner groupthink, including kinship bonding, presented problems.

It didn't matter whether it had been a family change—a new generation coming to management maturity in a closely held business— or someone coming in from the outside to take over a vital management position. The message was the same: All fellow presidents struggled with their CEO/board relationships as they tried to either make the legacy of their predecessors work to their advantage or tried to minimize the problems from the previous generations' CEO/board relationships which had created a groupthink situation.

There seemed to be three features of the YPO agenda that were familiar to all members. The first was the *owners' objectives*, and their degree of control in achieving those goals were primary sensitive points. Short-term vision and groupthink that initially energizes a small entrepreneurial venture can also begin to cripple a company as it expands beyond infancy. There comes a time when planning replaces instinct as a company looks toward long-term expansion. The owners who cannot make that transition pose a topside dilemma.

The second feature was *inertia* on the part of the owner/founder, or the decision (or, even tougher, the indecision) of the owner/founder to step aside when his or her most productive use to the company had come to an end. The causes were many, including groupthink and mindguards, and usually provoked unpleasant situations. How do you tell your leader that he's leaving, that the company's current posture demands a different kind of leadership than the entrepreneurial drive that got it going? It's a particularly thorny issue for small family businesses. Substitute "Dad" for "leader" in the previous question and you begin to get an idea of the sensitive issues involved.

The third feature on the agenda was the *clash of internal cultures*. The family system—often through the intervention of outside investors who had come to the board by reason of friendship with the founder—would collide with the business system, the boardroom professionals who brought the disciplines the company would need to reach its next plateau of growth.

The new chief executive has to learn from the old. Decisions have to be practical and objective rather than emotional and supportive. Respect has to take the place of groupthink camaraderie as the glue that holds the board and company together. And the CEO who comes out on top after change must take on the difficult task of filtering board relationships based on lineage through a fine screen of new respect deriving from professional standards, values, and authority.

Change may be triggered by normal career-cycle changes, a realignment following a merger, acquisition, or spin-off, or unsatisfactory financial performance. When such occasions arise, the power balance between the chief executive and the board often needs adjustment—needs the insertion of that modulator—to allow for the transfer of leadership or for a change in competitive conditions.

Birdcage management is how one Connecticut CEO describes the confusion of a company that grows from one plateau to the next. "When it is time to shake things up, all the birds fly around and land on different perches." To put a harder point on the analogy, the cage doors remain open during that shake-up. Some fly away, others collapse ineffectively onto the bottom of the cage.

A NEW COMPACT FOR OWNERS AND DIRECTORS

For years the process was simple. The CEO anointed his replacement and decided on the timing—all very quiet, all very private, all very insensitive in the use of power. In recent years, however, institutional investors and shareholder activists are forcing boards to take a more open, more public, and more responsible position on CEO succession.

In early 1990, a group of American attorneys organized an eight-member team called the Working Group on Corporate Governance. Its mandate was to provide guidelines for the balance between the CEO and his board. The result, "A New Compact for Owners and Directors," appeared the following year in the *Harvard Business Review.* Briefly, the report's recommendations included outside-board-member evaluation of CEO performance against regularly established goals, a suggestion that outside directors should meet at least once a year—a session coordinated by one of the outsiders—to evaluate the CEO as well as the process and flow of information between the executive office and the board, establishment of board-member qualifications, and a formal procedure for outside directors to screen and recommend future board members on the basis of qualifications established by the full board. The proposed compact is still being debated.

This model appears to presume a business world in which there are only a few special interests, few private agendas, and no issues of cronyism or groupthink. In a real world situation, one CEO in the financial services sector was not so lucky. He had come to his job from a new holding company that was intent on installing its own management group and changing the mind-set of the senior management. He arrived with his own diagnosis and prescription. "Some of the board members were very clear and willing to give me the time and space to do what was needed," he says. "For the most part, I was lucky enough to have people who were really good about it. They understood that, while they might want to spend more time managing, in fact, that was not their role."

To make topside changes effective, the CEO says, "You need to convey your feel for the company to the directors deepening their understanding. This is particularly important for those directors who come from the parental mind-set. They are going to be your advocates, so they need to be imbued with as much a feel for the company as possible. Even if they don't know every detail, you want them to have a gut-level comprehension of the company because there is always something that comes up in an odd moment that they are going to have to respond to. To do that well, they have to have a feel for the company."

This chief executive used his experience to identify that "feel" and recruited a board that could understand the culture and avoid mindguards and groupthink. "I was there at the beginning of the process," he explains, "and tried to bring the two companies closer, without stifling the creativity of the company that made it what it was. The fact is, the two needed to become closer. There is nothing worse than a company that is left sitting out there by itself. I'm not suggesting that everything become one, but you have to build the links between management and the board."

COMPETING MIND-SETS IN A
CLOSELY HELD COMPANY

In some instances, the problems of miscommunication start at the top. This is stated by James N. Farley, president of Famtec International Inc., in Des Plaines, Illinois, a thirty-seven-year-old holding company with principal operations in Europe and most major markets in the Far East.

Farley allows, "We call ourselves the smallest global company," and it was just that smallness that made its life complicated, if not out-and-out embarrassing. The company he joined in 1960 was entrepreneurially driven. When he signed on to handle sales, he purchased 35 percent of the company's shares. The board consisted of the owner/founder, Farley, and their two wives "making all the decisions in the back seat of a car going down the highway at 60 miles an hour." Groupthink was not at all complicated.

Famtec, which began business by manufacturing a critical semiconductor component, was driven by its founder's zeal in its early days and it prospered. When the company began to grow beyond its roots by moving into international markets and by taking on marketing as well as manufacturing, its needs for management skills changed. It was Farley who led the change. Or so he thought.

In the early 1970s, the founder decided to step aside. He cut his ownership back to 55 percent. A few years later, the founder became restless and decided he wanted to return and run the business. Says Farley, "War was declared. He voted his 55 percent, deciding Mr. Farley didn't need to be involved in the company and he was going to run the company." Even though "all but one of the minority shareholders decided they would rather have me run it than him," that 55 percent still was powerful. In the absence of any clear mandate, the company's bylaws kicked in. Both Farley and his founder had three loyal board members. In case of a deadlock, Farley related, "The president was the deciding person and I was, at the time, the president. We calmly locked him out of his office. We calmly declared war."

It was not a pleasant time for Farley or any members of the Famtec management. "They were beleaguered and more upset than I was. They didn't have any money and they worried about the company disappearing."

Both disputing parties hired separate counsel. Though his lawyers informed Farley that on a scale of one to ten, they were about an eleven on the measure of divorce bitterness, it worked. A management buyout was on the table within six months. The entire situation was resolved eight months later. "We bought the founder out over a five- or six-year period," Farley says. "He remained on the board for two or three years, as stipulated by the agreement. He came to board meetings, said nothing, did nothing, and left. There were no personal problems."

With a more secure management team, the company resumed its path of maturation. It added new board members, one a Japanese businessman, the other a general manager of a large Chicago production facility, and the third a professor from Northwestern University who specialized in small business—people to hold his feet to the fire. Farley says that they were "at the point where the promotional literature says the company is changing from the entrepreneurial to the managed business." Or so he thought.

There still was one director, the company's former number two management officer, who remained loyal to the old ways of doing business. He had resisted expansion and claimed that U.S. market share had been sacrificed to finance growth abroad. Famtec was in a bind. As a result of the management buyout, this executive had received some 20 percent of the company's stock. And, should Farley have "dropped dead," as he puts it, the retired number two would become a quite active number one with 51 percent of the company's stock.

"We decided to bite the bullet," Farley says, and the restructuring was, at long last, complete. The former manager was bought out but allowed to keep his seat on the board. "He is helpful and I didn't want him to be unhelpful. He is the real historian—someone who, besides me, can tell the story of how we got here." And his role has been restricted to such story-telling.

Instead of groupthink-type decisions made on interstate highways, Famtec has the balance of a sophisticated CEO and an intelligent board of directors. But that change has not come without some cost. Farley explains, "The entrepreneur says, 'Here's the flag. I'm going there. You guys follow me. If you get into trouble, let me know and I'll get you out of it. You just pick up the papers and back me up.' That doesn't work anymore. We've switched to a more organized professional management, and we have lost some people. They couldn't keep up. You say to them, 'You help tell us where we want to go. You're responsible for getting us there.' It didn't work. We had a couple of people who quit, a couple we had to buy out. But the board seems to understand that it's all part of the company's topside change."

While he retains absolute control of the company with 80 percent of its stock, Farley appreciates that he has people on his board who will tell him what they think. "I don't really sit down with them and discuss what's going on in the company on a day-to-day basis," he says. "I keep them informed on what a board should know."

The directors, in turn, keep him apprised of how they react to the information. The culture is anything but groupthink. Rather, it is professionalthink. Farley says that the college professor and the production manager, in particular, want to know what better financing programs the company might pursue. He says, "They want to know if we are growing strictly for sales alone. Or if we might be outgrowing our banking. They are strong board members in that they speak up and say, 'You're not doing it right.'"

In a decade of seemingly continual topside change, Farley was able to rely on the advice of an independent board that was built to suit the company's need for varied expertise and his own need for support and counsel. And because that board is never afraid to speak up and demand that Farley adjust his course of action, he'll never have to worry about finding his replacement before he's ready to make the change.[1]

Devil's Advocate

The proverb, "Advice when most needed is least heeded," holds for many organizations. Unfortunately, some boards do not enter-tain independent viewpoints inconsistent with the group's beliefs. Such a devil's advocate role of independent directors on a board needs to be encouraged. It is yet to be an enforceable role in director behavior. Formalizing this dissent role, however, is as old as history itself. Within the Roman Catholic Church, the devil's advocate, formally termed "promoter of the faith," has been a continuing functional office since the early 1500s. The prescribed function in the Church is to thoroughly investigate proposals for canonization and beatification.

In the Church context, the devil's advocate must bring to light any information that might cast doubt on the qualifications of a candidate for sainthood. Organizational separation of the functions of promoter and dissenter thus ensures that both sides of the question are thoroughly analyzed and presented. The process works, despite some occasional imperfections. (One cynical observer characterized the devil's advocate as a prosecuting attorney, retained to see that a potential saint is holy inadequate.)

In our Anglo-Saxon legal system, the dissenting function is also formalized. Jury and judge examine the merits of the prosecution's case and the counterproposal by the defense's presentation. The system allows airing of the positive and negative sides of questions. Our corporate governance system, perhaps, could improve with similar formal emphasis on the devil's advocate process.

So far, many business corporations, closely held and publicly held, do not uniformly match this dissenting function technique in their board process. Yet they still get on with their primary task. Applying the devil's advocate concept in the boardroom is tricky, particularly when the board is dominantly an insider or a family board. Volunteering criticism of a fellow family or managing director can be taken as a personal attack. As a result, open, constructive criticism may be withheld. One medium-sized, family-owned, national service firm that I know fell into the practice of family directors, employing a "your turn to get approval" technique in the boardroom. This avoidance practice developed to a point where the company's growth was stalemated because of political maneuvering amongst board members.

One obvious organizational risk to the devil's advocate role is undue reliance on outside expertise. This ignores the judgment of those in the firm who know the business best. A careful balance between expert input by independent directors (or advisors) and the input of those held accountable for actions and proposals needs to be considered carefully and continuously. Morale, retention of key people, and development of a belief in equitable, realistic, and fair governance decision making and accountability are at stake.

Directors can't be perfect when risking groupthink bias. They can, however, avoid mindguards by common sense enforcement of a better balance of inputs and openness as the basis for judgment in decision making.

Behavioral Theory and Groupthink

The notion of economic man assumes rational decision making. This doesn't dock neatly with the concept of us as human beings or social actors capable of managing our own environment. The issue of social responsibility and the realities of human behavior become and always have been the ultimate determinance of sound decision making. Human thinking and behavior, however, are not always rational. There is the classical clash between the rational economic man thesis and the nonrational, noneconomic, emotional, value-oriented social man thesis.[2]

The board is expected to govern by rational decision making. However, the public perceives business corporations as quasi-public institutions with responsibilities that include, but also transcend, the purely economic. The public is concerned not only with what companies do and how they do it but also with the manner in which their role in society is defined and fundamental policies are set.

Scholars have pointed out that we should not neglect the fact that man's reason has, at most, a secondary and small influence upon his conduct. Irrational or nonrational feelings and desires are the real causes of nearly all of men's actions.

A more perceptive thesis has been offered by scholars that our normal state is one in which behavior is not purposive, is noncalculative, is governed by emotions and values, is potentially inconsistent and conflict ridden, and is indifferent to defense. It suggests also that our normal state is under the influence of groupthink.

The cost of being rational can be put another way. According to psychologists, nonrational behavior is natural; rational conduct is artificial, must be manufactured, and has a cost. The fact that resources must be sacrificed to gain rationality provided empirical evidence that rational behavior is a product. From an individual director's perspective, to seek one's goals costs the commitment of resources, energy, time, and dedication. Emotional investment is required. Self-discipline, moderation of self-interest, or sense of collectivity is involved.

Given the fact that there is no accepted theory of governance, that no two boards are alike, and that there is no perfect board, the balance between economic and social man is a hard one to maintain. Perfection in this juggling act is hard to come by, if at all.

2

Limitations to Live With: Directors Don't Have to Be Perfect

He lacked only a few vices to be perfect.
Marquise de Sévigné (1626–1696)
French Lady of Fashion and Letter Writer

A perfect director is one whose greatest flaw is his or her inability to accept a flawed world. It has also been said that those directors who think they are perfect are very annoying to those of us who are. Flaws and imperfections aside, we must recognize certain limitations all directors live with in order to be effective.

The real difference between turkeys and eagles on boards is not perfection but concerns professionalism, relevant experience, integrity, commitment, and communications ability. These are the vital attributes for a director to be effective in the corporate briar patch of governance.

There are over 200 orthogonal variables and many theories identified by scholars for the realm of management. However, there is no accepted theory of governance. Furthermore, the issues enveloped in effectiveness as a board member are specific to a company. Issues also vary somewhat by industry and by legal-regulatory circumstances extant in a national or regional area. Let's look back at some history.

In 1912, the Olympic, predecessor sister ship of the Titanic, was designed by the Right Honorable Alexander Carlisle who remembered a board meeting where lifeboat capacity was discussed "for five or ten minutes," whereas the time allotted for the discussion of decorations for the liners ran up to five hours. Managing agenda time is an unenforceable process but a vital one.

This tragic incident reminds me of the cartoon quip of a chairman to one of his officers, "We've got a dummy corporation here, what we need is a smarty corporation." If you substitute board of directors for corporation, you have the essence of this boardroom happening.

There are more recent imperfect events. For example, a July 8, 1993 article in the *Wall Street Journal* (WSJ) concerned ethics in business. It was entitled, "The Accidental Facts Ethics Case." The lawyer received a revealing memo from his opposing counsel, courtesy of the latter's bumbling clerk. What do you do with it? One option is to use the information without hesitation. Another is that Virginia law requires lawyers to use the information. A third option is that the American Bar Association (ABA) counsels return the information without reading it. This may be unrealistic. Certainly it's virtuous and unenforceable.

From a personal conduct ethics test standpoint, I always use the following three questions: (1) Is it legal? (2) Can I explain to my family why I made a decision? and (3) How would I feel if the information came out in the local paper in the morning? This WSJ event concerned applied ethics, not philosophical ethics. A decision includes the concepts of servanthood without dominance, obedience to the unenforceable, and the tone-at-the-top of the organization.

In dealing with such an "anguished ethics" decision, directors are inherently in the comic position of carrying water from wells that they haven't dug to fight fires that they can't quite find. Business ethical dilemmas are especially vexatious. They concern the process of making an ethical decision at three different levels, namely, the personal level, the organizational level, and the level in which society surrounds the corporation.

Here is another example of imperfect events. In August 1993, a reporter from the *Toledo Blade* interviewed me on the subject of business ethics. This was a background inquiry to aid in his coverage of an active court case being tried in the courts (and in the press) in which directors of an American subsidiary of a British-owned company had allegedly created a structure of peripheral subsidiaries which did business with the company. The matter concerned conflict of interest in the eyes of the prosecutor—a violation of the duty of loyalty.

The reporter wanted to know how pervasive this activity was in the world of corporate governance with an implication that most boards behave in this way. My reply stressed the significance of such imperfect behavior and the statistical infrequency of this in the world of corporate governance. In the United States, professional groups, private-sector companies, and academic communities are hard at work in defining what is the proper board behavior.

Another example is that earlier this year, a business editor from a large, well-known, New York publishing house contacted Arthur D. Little, Inc., in search of an author for a new book on the subject of board empowerment. The editor wrote the following:

The recent publicity regarding GM and the action of its board gave me an idea for a book. The premise of this book is that the corporate boards are going to have to take a more pro-active role in running the company. The days of rubber stamping CEO decisions are over; boards need to run the business and take action when action is necessary. I see this book as being something like *Corporate Board Empowerment*, with a subtitle like *A Blueprint for Action and Survival Guide for the Director*. Case studies and references like IBM and other notorious boards would be added.

Obviously, the editor was uninformed about the relationship between the latent power of the board, the kinetic power of the executive management, and the appropriate process for balancing these powers.

A final example of imperfect events involves the Presidents Association of American Management Association's recently published special study entitled, "Boardworthiness: From a President's and a Director's Perspective."[1] Chapter 1 was titled, "A Director's Do-It-Yourself Checkup: Are You Boardworthy for the 1990s?" Thirteen attribute categories were in my checklist, including competence, applied ethics, and independence, plus a self-rating matrix as to "honors," "pass," or "fail." These self-examination guidelines signified that an honors rating implied that the director's service was one of distinction, meaning overall high effectiveness. Pass ratings implied the director's performance was satisfactory on essentially all counts. Fail ratings means the director is unacceptably deficient in contribution, performance, or effectiveness. The self-rating covered a wide range of perfection to imperfection. The checklist is included in this book as Appendix A.

The "checkup" was a suggested thought process not meant to be constraining or overly quantitative. Response from readers showed considerable interest. Almost everyone said that when they took the test themselves it was near impossible to pass on all honors for the attributes. I must admit that these were drawn up with that thought-provoking concern in mind. Only "water walkers" would be able to have honors in terms of my boardworthiness checkup. See Appendix A for applications of this checkup.

It is true that half of life's experiences are below average in satisfaction and certainly in perfection. But as a boardroom buff I can say from my own boardroom exposure that there is no substitute for genuine lack of preparation for directorship. The purpose of this anchoring point is to stress the fact that it may be unattainable to be a perfect or proper director. However, that is no excuse for not trying to be one.

THE PERSONAL SIDE OF BOARDROOM CONDUCT[2]

My big business board debut occurred in 1961 with election to Monsanto's board and executive committee. I was "housemother" to the eighty-nine subsidiaries and affiliates around the world. This provided a fascinating opportunity to find out what goes on behind the boardroom door in different cultures and foreign situations. My views were developed from the bias of an inside director. But what I learned from the conduct and thinking of the dominant number of outside directors on the Monsanto and subsidiary boards made me appreciate the value of independent, objective input to the boardroom.

Some say that anyone who accepts election to a publicly owned U.S. company board does not know enough about exposures and liabilities to be qualified. But for those who do seek or accept an invitation to join a board, some of the following axioms may help:

1. No matter how much of a dividend is declared by a board of directors or how significant an acquisition, restructuring, divestiture, or merger may be, some of the shareowners will not like it.

2. No matter how trivial a capital expenditure investment may be, it's always possible to build it up into a major expansion as far as competition is concerned.

3. Emeritus directors will attend all meetings regardless of the weather, the agenda, or the inconvenience. There will be the same old faces, but a lot of new teeth.

4. The less important or younger you are on a board of directors, the more you will be missed if you do not show up for a meeting. Some directors have to be stuck with committee work.

5. Three boardroom crises occur with the owners of closely held corporations: (1) the crisis of letting go; (2) the crisis of reorganization; and (3) the crisis of succession—the dynastic tendency.

When a chairman perceives that the company needs vital help, remember Erma Bombeck's rule of medicine, "Never go to a doctor whose office plants have died." Strengthen the board externally and its management internally with some experienced, credible professionals who can focus attention on the key survival and development issues.

I have learned through many years in industry and consulting that the elusive concept of governance and management requires more of a sociological/behavioral perspective for the individual director. This embodies a perceptive, intuitive, simultaneous, and qualitative viewpoint—the high-touch side of the governance equation with which most lawyers are quite familiar. Many directors' backgrounds are in the high-tech side, however.

At the board level, there is also difficulty in balancing the disciplinary, command-control-communication management side with the growth-development-innovative-visionary governance side of the equation. This is where I perceive that there is an unsatisfied requirement for more leadership from those knowledgeable in jurisprudence, sociology, and political science. Here is a particular area where those educated in law can assist the CEO and help the board think through vexatious issues and problems.

A few years ago, I attended a bank board meeting where we were considering increasing a seven-figure line of credit to one of Boston's prime not-for-profit performing arts organizations, the Boston Ballet, a $3- to $4-million turnover corporation. The ballet characteristically runs a deficit that is collateralized by a large endowment. The annual deficit is covered by socially prominent donors each year. The popular *Nutcracker*, traditionally offered at Christmastime, brings in the most revenues. Most other presentations usually lose money.

The classical confrontation of business management with creative management was vividly present in this situation. One anecdote was told of the choreographer and art director wanting twelve toe dancers for a scene in *Romeo and Juliet*. The business manager's solution was to use seven and move them around a lot! The management dilemma was how to retain the aesthetic and artistic fuel that drives and distinguishes the Boston Ballet yet still have management control over cost.

Those of us who make our living in business rather than ballet have the same dilemma in distinguishing between managing and governing. There is also the problem of increasing external complexity and turmoil in the political, social, and economic environment in which we must conduct our activities.

The simple answers to being an effective if not a perfect director is that we must fulfill the legal and regulatory requirements—directors are required to legitimatize the corporation (every corporation must have a board of directors). Then we must audit the performance of the company, in particular its financial matters. Finally, we must provide informed oversight and monitoring of the corporation's and the CEO's performance.

Limitations Directors Must Cope With

Corporate governance concepts and processes are currently undergoing transformation to adapt to changes in the following: (1) the role and nature of boards; (2) the boundary or compass of board concerns; (3) board structure and board processes; and (4) board renewal and development. These dynamics are evolutionary and company specific. Changes are often subtle. How to make directors pay attention to these issues and strive in their search for perfection is a challenge. There are at least eight limitations with which directors must learn to cope.

Limitation One—Boardroom Boundaries   Boards of directors tend to draw boundaries around their domain with more dogmatism than experience or good conduct warrants—boundaries between the board and management or between the corporation and its environment. Boards are often closed systems similar to the command and control, closed-system characteristic of the conventionally structured management system. A board is perceived to be a closed domain, but it must be open to opportunity in relation to the outside world.

Limitation Two—Board Nature Many boards do not explicitly allow for the often bewildering options open to directors and the decisions they face in governing a corporation. In many cases there is no one right answer to a problem or a question requiring the board's resolution. It is often the wisest course to offer a fix that recognizes that a decision will not be carved in stone, will not please anyone totally, but will recognize and allow for the ambiguity of a given solution.

A study published in 1980—James Brian Quinn's *Strategies for Change: Logical Incrementalism* (Richard D. Irwin)—of ninety senior executives, interviewed at General Mills, Pillsbury, EXXON, Continental Group, Xerox, Pilkington, General Motors, Chrysler, and Volvo, revealed an explicit rationale for leaving strategic pronouncements in a somewhat fuzzy state. The respondents preferred ambiguity in strategic declarations to avoid undesired centralization, focusing otherwise fragmented opposition, rigidity, which closes down options and makes explicit goals hard to change, and breaches of security on sensitive plans.

Limitation Three—Board Life Cycles All boards have a life cycle of their own. The stage of the life cycle represented by the board's condition may not be congruent with the life cycles of the corporation served or the strategic business unit involved in the diversified enterprise. Board life cycle depends on the nature and composition of board membership and the respective maturity and group experience of directors working together. Within the boardroom, directors have either an explicit or implicit contract (or conflict) with others within the collective unit. This relationship is either a social, intellectual, or emotional contract, or a mix of these. As a consequence, directors are bound together by sharing the same fate of directing an institution as stewards, trustees, or fiduciaries in an uncertain environment. The problem with some boards is that they are in a declining state of effectiveness and inaction is the consequence. They often act like the planning committee for the Annual Conference of Clairvoyants when they canceled their meeting because of unforeseen circumstances.

Limitation Four—Board Renewal   Membership renewals, succession, and continuity of a board of directors are as vital as an effective management development process. Unfortunately, director recruitment, education, development, evaluation, separation, and succession are sometimes neglected processes. The only practice worse than this neglect is when a board pursues things they never should have started.

The plain facts are that the role of the board is often unclear and not fully accepted in many situations. Crises, takeovers, and succession struggles are the usual exceptions. The conventional functions of governance generally described as legitimatizing, oversight, monitoring, auditing, and general strategic direction are often dominated by stronger management or owner interests.

Separation of governance from management through a well-defined role for the board is yet to be universally and realistically accepted in many firms. This is particularly true of closely held corporations, small- and medium-sized companies where stakeholder or commonweal interests may not yet be fully acknowledged.

Limitation Five—Board Process   The researcher's motto, "If we knew what we were doing it wouldn't be research," fits here. In the boardroom, if we knew the answers, we wouldn't be governing. Governance processes do not necessarily match those processes which are most effective in resolving issues in the management realm. Board functions differ significantly from those of management. The latter are hierarchically oriented. Management decision processes are judicial and directive in nature with allocation of power and accountability.

Governance, in contrast, is achieved in a nonhierarchical form. Political processes and peer processes are at work in the boardroom. Consensus is strived for. Differences in opinion are (or should be) encouraged. Meshing this governance process with the management process requires "a system of systems" to provide proper operational linkage of the systems for financial control, strategic decisions, power flow, and information feedback.

Limitation Six—The Temporal Dimension   Boards seem to be occupied with what is, for the present or for the short-term future. Many tend to confirm the status quo. But time and tide wait for no board; the need for timely governance persists. The board is particularly concerned with the future consequences of present corporate decisions.

Limitation Seven—Board Score   Boards do not often study or objectively examine the more elusive, ineffable, noncommensurable attributes of the domain of corporate governance. Characterizing, assessing, and evaluating plenary board effectiveness (and individual director effectiveness) are both formidable and delicate tasks. The limitation is that it is nobody's business to do the rating, except perhaps in those instances which the chairman is also the CEO and an important stockholder in his or her own right. In most companies, the board and the CEO are both creators of the other to an extent. As a result, it is presumptuous for either to advance complicated ideas about the inevitable qualities of the board's activities.

Limitation Eight—Learning   A director's personal mechanisms of perception and cognition basically operate to limit sensory input so the individual can make sense of the data-rich world. An awareness of the experience and opinion of others also influences a director toward sensory input which is compatible with others' experience. This is what you get when you are expecting something else.

These learning processes serve a director by creating consistent frameworks from which to view the world and determine how to conduct one's self in it. Learning is involved as the organizing framework and is modified to account for repeated exposure to experience not in accord with the original tenets of an individual director.

More formal learning situations are becoming fashionable for directors. Universities, colleges, professional associations, trade associations, consulting firms, and publishing houses have jumped into the director seminar and corporate governance education field.

PEER POWER AND PERFECTION

Peer power has existed, of course, from the time of primitive man. It appears in varied and unexpected ways in our daily existence. It is certainly at work in the boardroom. Peer power is obviously a substantial factor in business, academic, military, scientific, and governance domains.

Peer Evaluations at the Naval Academy

I was initially surprised to hear of the abandoning of peer evaluations at the Naval Academy through some personal three-way correspondence with James F. Calvert, Vice Admiral, USN (Retired), and Robert W. McNitt, Rear Admiral, USN (Retired), Dean of Admissions, United States Naval Academy, Annapolis, Maryland.

It was the opinion of the responsible officers that peer evaluations had some value if used only once or twice but rapidly lost validity if continued for a long period of time. Evaluations did not change much over several years, and there was some concern that a low rating initially could become a self-fulfilling prophecy. To quote Admiral McNitt, "The elimination of peer evaluations has had no significant adverse effects and has been very popular with midshipmen. A third of the Brigade Officers felt that there was a loss of useful data, but that it was not worth the effort required to obtain it; another third felt that there was not an appreciable effect. One sixth of the officers felt that there was appreciable loss of useful data from the elimination of peer evaluations and another sixth recommended a partial return to the use of peer evaluations."

Peer ratings are used both as predictors and as criterion measures, although the latter use is not very encouraging. Operational use of peer ratings as criterion measures in the Navy, Army, metropolitan police forces, and board of directors is considered somewhat premature.

Use of peer ratings as predictors of performance has had some impressive success, although it is no longer employed at the Naval Academy. I agree with the Naval Academy findings that reuse of this type of rating is not warranted. It presents other problems even beyond the potential self-fulfilling prophecy problem cited by Admiral McNitt.

Some of these complicating problems are the role of friendship, subgroup (clique) formation, stereotypes, and implicit theories of personality. These disadvantage new persons introduced to the intact group or board, and there is difficulty in understanding peer ratings before using them formally. Despite these problems, the greatest untapped potential for use of peer ratings is as a source of performance feedback. This is a tricky process to use in an acceptable manner for most groups and particularly for a board of directors.

The use of peer ratings as a source of performance feedback is now being used effectively on at least two boards where I have participated—one college board and one chemical industry company board—through the mechanism of the organization committee of the board. Annual peer reviews of members of the board are informally but rigorously carried out by the outside-director committee members, the chairman, and the chief executive. Some directors have been allowed to resign after negative ratings; others have shaped up their interest and attendance after a low peer rating.

Peer Power and the Ex-Scion President

Ten years ago I served on a financial intermediary company board made up of eighteen male directors, most of whom were Midwesterners but four of whom were from the East. Three were local businessmen in the city where this company was headquartered. One was the chief executive of a small chain of family-owned retail supermarkets in the Midwest. The market chain was bought out, and the scion-president found himself further enriched but out of a job. He devoted his time to charitable organizations in the community where he distinguished himself in lending some management expertise to not-for-profit groups.

He neglected to stay in touch with the rapidly changing business world. After three years of being out of the stream of business activity, his contributions to our board waned to a pitiful level, though his social presence and insight remained respectably high. The committee of his peers on the board were charged with nomination and renomination of director candidates. They decided he should not remain on the board despite the public and personal relationships that might suffer from dropping a well-respected member of the community.

Advising him of this evaluation caused some internal fireworks, but the committee and the chairman held firm. He was not renominated. Social and personal ruptures in the community took place as he was dropped out of the director caste. In the last three years, this local tension has abated somewhat, but the correct deed was done for the benefit of the shareowners. The replacement director is an active economist from an international banking firm who brings current insight to the board meetings. The moral is, "It's not what time you put in but what you put in the time." While there was an orderly—if delicate—show of peer power, peer support is vain, political, and unpredictable. It's liable to leave you high and dry just when it's most needed.

Peer Criteria for the Proper Director

The most effective peer evaluation method I have used in counselling boards of directors is an effectiveness rating scheme developed on an assignment with a century-old, London-based, multinational company. Individual directors were judged by seven subjective attributes on a rating scale of one point for "deficient in performance or effectiveness," two points for "satisfactory on most counts," and three points for "director service of distinction."

Confidential ratings of ten individual fellow directors were made orally to me in private interviews with each of the eleven directors. All were promised anonymity in return for a candid rating of their boardroom companions on the following generally agreed-upon criteria for a proper director (a much better term than a perfect director). The seven attributes are as follows:

1. Professional performance as a director over a sustained period by providing significant and useful inputs to the board
2. Character and integrity above reproach, along with keen perspective and the ability to make good judgments
3. Balanced leadership contributions (including good attendance, active interest, and support to the company and its board)
4. Sustained business or professional development and achievement for the purpose of helping the company's strategy, marketing efforts, and stakeholders relationships
5. Creates a natural following, interpersonal rapport, and peer respect from other board members and top management
6. Has sincere interest in board and management succession and in staff development
7. Provides special services, such as distinguished contributions or special insights into the company, namely, public service recognition, recruiting of "stars," and novel business ideas for corporate development

These seven points were weighed on a one-two-three scale and then composited to get a consensus score, with the range indicated, for each director as confidentially judged by his boardroom mates. Then, I prepared a matrix display of ten fellow director ratings without individual attribution of each member of the board. This subjective judgmental rating was discussed privately with each director to let him or her know not how I rated his conduct but how his fellow directors perceived his boardworthiness.

These dance-of-the-seven-veils attributes proved to be an electric shock treatment to at least three of the directors. They were rated one and one-half (less than satisfactory) on balanced leadership, business or professional development, and interpersonal rapport. The evaluations were never used except in my individual counselling session with each director and with the chairman. No one was given details on who rated whom and at what level, but each was given the composite standing of his fellow directors as judged by their respective companion.

I kept track (privately) of the individual directors evaluated for about six years. With no exceptions, individual directorship improved dramatically. Two lagging directors were fortunately dropped when a business conflict developed. The board is now swinging and swaying with a sense of achievement and camaraderie not present before. They haven't reached perfection, but they are closer to it!

Pulling off such a confidential rating task can only be done when there is a level of trust and experience mutually shared by the counsellor and the individual board members. Giving that level of trust may be a good technique for upgrading effectiveness of a board of directors.

Given these seven criteria for a proper, rather than a perfect, director, it is appropriate to conclude with the statement of Samuel Butler (1835–1902), English novelist and satirist, who opined, "If you aim at imperfection, there is some chance of you getting it; whereas if you aim at perfection there is none."

3

The Oyster Not the Shell: Enterprise versus Corporation

An enterprise is not a corporation. A corporation is not an enterprise. Some enterprises are incorporated; some enterprises are not incorporated.

An enterprise is an assembly of human beings and economic resources organized for the production of goods and services. It is a complex culture of communication and control systems, loyalties, and disciplines—a functioning social organism. It obeys the statutory and common laws and regulations and the unenforceable canons, norms, and relationships resting on shared commitment to ideas, issues, goals, and governance and management processes. These latter relationships concern covenantal matters, or agreements between people.

A corporation is a doctrinal concept in the law. It is a legal format, one of a number of legal formats that a lawyer may select to wrap around an enterprise. A corporation is only a lawyer-made carapace that surrounds an enterprise. It is prescribed by the domain of positive law and regulations.

A corporation is no more an enterprise than an oyster shell is an oyster. The enterprise is an economic entity that produces something. The corporation produces nothing. The corporation is the domain of lawyers, accountants, and, latterly, investment bankers. The enterprise is the domain of business executives and leaders.

Most platform talk and literature about governance thoughtlessly mixes up corporate governance and enterprise governance as though they were interchangeable. They are not. What's worse is that most such discussions, by some perverse accident, are so cast as to imply that the important public policy issues involved relate to corporate governance. The truth is to the contrary.

The preceding intellectual rationale was presented to the World Management Congress at the Waldorf-Astoria Hotel in New York City on September 21, 1989. According to Bayless Manning, the speaker on that occasion and former dean of Stanford Law School, the truly big issues that confront us relate to enterprise governance.[1]

This point of view is an anchoring point for director judgment and knowledge. It assists in understanding the contractual and particularly the covenantal relationships discussed. These concern the difference between the human enterprise oyster and the legal structure or shell of an enterprise. Statutory and common laws and the regulatory framework provide degrees of freedom, constraints, boundaries, and systems for the corporate carapace in which the human system, or oyster, enterprise is located.

The heart of Moulton's Manners—obedience to the unenforceable, as described in the section called Moulton's Manners at the beginning of the book—is the enterprise and its nature, identity, processes, ethical practice, relationships, and organizational learnings.

Oyster-shell models are more structured. The geometry is often complex. Both intentionally and unintentionally, it mixes up corporate and other legal business structures. This is in response to competition, tax obligations, legal and regulatory controls, public profile, and ownership objectives.

THE HOLLOW CORPORATION

Business Week's Special Report Edition, March 3, 1986, emblazoned this title across its magazine cover in Second Coming typeface. It trumpeted a new kind of company evolving in the United States: manufacturing companies that do little manufacturing. Instead, they import components or products from low-wage countries, slap their own names on them, and sell them in America. Unchecked, say the editors, this outsourcing trend will ultimately hurt the economy by retarding productivity, innovation, and the standard of living.

Akio Morita, Sony Corporation chairman and cofounder, apparently provoked this characterization with the following arresting statement: "American companies have either shifted output to low-wage countries or come to buy parts and assembled parts from countries like Japan that can make quality products at low prices. The result is the hollowing of American industry. The U.S. is abandoning its status as an industrial power." This globalization wave of industrial and service company migration from the United States spawned many archetypes of corporate architecture, including network cliques, syndicates, alliances, host-corps, joint ventures, federations, partnerships, and coalitions. Such proliferation often exacerbates the boundary confusion between governance and management.

The contractual obligations are spelled out in the respective sovereign formats, all tied to the contractual or legal shell. The oyster essence of these structural archetypes relies on the social contract model of one or more small societies represented by the enterprise.

The social contract model and its business target market may be viewed as a small society in an anthropological sense. This implies groups of unequal beings organized to meet common objectives and needs. A social contract is sought in each society (oyster enterprise) in order to achieve its objectives and needs. Such a contract is defined as having sufficient order to protect the members of the enterprise. In addition, there is sufficient disorder to provide every individual with full opportunity to develop his genetic endowment, whatever that may be, in a free enterprise society. In particular, the freedom to fail characterizes the risk factors.

The social contract model recognizes that a society of equals is an impossibility—each oyster enterprise has its own character and existence. However, our free enterprise, democratic philosophy, structures, and context set forth the assertion that a just society, with social, contractual, and covenantal linkages, is a realizable goal. This presumes responsible obedience to the unenforceable.

The balance of order and disorder varies in vigor and effectiveness in any partnership of governance and management of an enterprise. The balance depends on the environmental circumstances. It seeks a continual dynamic equilibrium. In this respect, a framework of legal and social norms, as anchoring points, shape the learning potentials, the initiatives, the relationships, and the cooperation.

CORPORATE FORM FOLLOWS FUNCTION

The legal concept of incorporating an entrepreneurial enterprise was developed in the late 1800s. In this oyster/oyster-shell model, the investor had unlimited upside possibility for profit, with a limitation of downside risk. The investor's interest was also transferable. This model was a vehicle for raising large amounts of capital, a stable structure for centralized management, and a continuity for the enterprise extending past the lives of natural persons.

In fact, one of Western history's most remarkable organization achievements became the large publicly owned enterprise governed by an independent board of directors. Evidence of the attraction of this model has never been more evident than in its adoption and experimentation by non-Western countries, undergoing political change in their transformations from command economies to market economies.

In the last several years I have had the opportunity to participate in consulting and educational assignments in various developing countries' programs for sustainable development. The corporate enterprise was a key concept and model form of strategic business initiatives.

Five of the engagements involved dealing with the formation and modification of private enterprise or parastatal enterprise programs to improve overall efficiency and productivity of the respective economies or selected business sectors. Examples can be seen in the following:

- World Bank financial programs of structural adjustment and public-enterprise reform in Egypt. The focus was on their privatization program, divestment of government-owned companies, and reform of the policy environment of the public-enterprise sector.

- Hungary's pioneer program of a market-driven economy preceding the U.S.S.R. upheaval. A major effort was initiated for assessing and training industrial top managers; it included conducting pilot seminars.

- Caribbean enterprise development, sponsored by the University of the West Indies as lead organization, to strengthen management education in the private sector, including seminars in Trinidad.

- China's awakened interest in free-enterprise management education, drawing on Western resources for orientation and education on private-enterprise formation and development.

- Bangladesh's continuing attack on population control and public health. This involves, *inter alia*, a unique social marketing concept utilizing a private corporation, later a parastatal form and recently a revamped corporate enterprise with improved governance and focused executive management. This enterprise provides (sells) services and products for birth spacing, preventing diahorreal disease, and birth control education.

CONTRASTS BETWEEN EASTERN AND WESTERN MANAGERS

In 1993, the American Management Association (AMA) conducted a research study in Central and Eastern Europe responding to the companies in the West which sensed an opportunity unique in modern history. The people east of the old Iron Curtain are culturally advanced, and their economies, though state controlled for three generations, are based (similarly to the West) upon industrial production and technological services, however they compare to Western standards. The concept of enterprise governance is novel in many Eastern European countries striving to compete with the West.

But in the new evolving Europe, the gulf between Eastern and Western management practices and concepts is vast. Entire management disciplines, such as finance, marketing, and even general management and governance, are not as well developed. Their practice bears little resemblance to familiar Western procedures.[2]

Even more vital are the interpersonal factors—the social contract features—when Western managers arrive in Central and Eastern Europe to organize and supervise a local management team in the free enterprise mode. Huge differences in work experience must be recognized and reconciled.

Research was based on interviews with Western managers assigned to enterprises in Hungary, Czechoslovakia, and Poland, and with Eastern managers at work in those same enterprises. While the economic and political conditions in Central and Eastern Europe do not compare with those in the Asia Pacific area, and in China specifically, the West and China do have two radically different economies and political conditions.

If, for example, a similar research study were made in China at the present time, undoubtedly there would be some parallel between the Western manager's viewpoint of doing business in China and the Chinese manager's experience in conducting business in the West. A most probable parallel might be difficulties in cooperation between managers with different economic and governance experiences of the two prospective political blocks. This includes differences in personal mentalities spawned by experiences of the executives in their respective economic, political, and cultural environments—the social contract, or oyster characteristics, of the business enterprise.

The difficulties that were most important out of seven identified, either from a Western manager or an Eastern manager's viewpoint, were different economic experience (54–76%), different mentality (57–76%), language comprehension (40–58%), and practical on-site problems (36–58%). Three other minor difficulties were shown in the survey but were substantially less than these four dominating ones. The minor ones were personal prejudices of either Eastern or Western managers and poor education of local managers. Note that from our anchoring point perspective, these difficulties concern the oyster and not the oyster shell.

Capitalistic ideology and the challenge of making boards and executive management more accountable is a hot topic in Western economies. Some characteristics are the following:[3]

- The impact of institutional investors. California Public Employees Retirement System (CALPERS) had forty-two companies in their portfolio between 1987–1992 which yielded an increase of 6.8 percent average increase above Standard & Poor's 500 Index returns. This improvement in return is attributable to CALPERS' influence with the boards of directors and executive management of the companies in their portfolio.

- The American–British brand of corporate governance emphasizes liquidity in the stockmarket. This makes it cheaper for companies to raise capital by reducing the risk that investors will be unable to sell their shares.

- The German–Japanese system plays down the liquidity for investors (many German companies are private, their shareholders illiquid). Shareholders reduce risks by monitoring managers closely or by having a trusted intermediary—a bank—do the monitoring on their behalf.

- In Japan and Germany the large shareowners are banks and firms which have business links with companies they own (the five biggest investors in General Motors own 9% of the firm; Daimler-Benz's top five shareowners own 68%).

This capitalistic ideology, the mixing up of corporate governance and enterprise governance (the oyster shell versus the oyster) is not confined to Western political regions. The *Financial Times* (February 21, 1994) included a brief report on China's fledgling stockmarkets which is of particular concern to this Asian context. Professor Li Yining, one of China's most influential economists and the head of a parliamentary committee drafting the new Securities Law, believes that additional steps to bolster public trust in capital markets are vital for market reforms. Most important, Professor Li sees the development of China's equity markets "as a means of facilitating a faltering process of corporatization and privatization. If we don't set up shareholding companies, we will never be able to separate government and management."

A century ago, Imperial China distinguished between "China's learning for essential matters" and "Western learning for practical matters." Today, it is both essential and practical to straighten out any confusion between corporate governance and enterprise governance. In the spirit of this anchoring point perspective, Professor Li might have added that it's the oyster and not the oyster shell that is the big issue.

4

The Covenantal Divide: Contractual versus Covenantal Relationships

Pocket picking is a recognized profession, and is highly unionized in Egypt. When King Farouk was married on January 20, 1938, the King of the Thieves issued a proclamation in the Cairo newspapers. He promised, as a friendly gesture to the other King, to call off all of his thieves during the nuptial celebrations. And not a pocket was picked! This covenantal proclamation was a self-imposed compact out of respect for the sovereign King, pledging to keep the notorious band of quick-change artists from picking their way through the celebrant crowds.

In ancient times, an earlier recorded theological covenant was an agreement made between Jehovah and his people of Israel, whereby Israel was to be faithful to Jehovah. Jehovah was to protect and bless his faithful people. The *quid pro quo* was a shared commitment.

THE GREAT DIVIDE IN DIRECTORSHIP

My boardroom service did not begin until 1952 when I served as president and a director of Shawinigan Resins Corporation in Indian Orchard, Massachusetts. The company was a joint business venture between Shawinigan Chemicals Ltd., a Canadian company, and Monsanto Company. No one told me then, nor anytime since with numerous directorships, that there was such a thing as a covenantal *quid pro quo* dimension to the role of corporate director.

Any orientation or education was focused on the legal and contractual side of corporate governance. But two perspectives, contractual and covenantal, are jointly important. The challenge is to recognize these divided sets of relationships and then close the gap between them to achieve a balance in decision making, conflict resolution, and trade-offs over matters of economic and social accountability.

Nobel Laureate Douglass C. North, professor of economics and history at Washington University in St. Louis, has recently extended his groundbreaking analysis of economic structures to develop an analytical framework to account for the survival of economies and institutions with persistently poor performance for very long periods of time. Institutions exist, he argues, due to uncertainties involved in human interaction; they are the constraints devised to structure that interaction.[1]

Professor North uses the distinction of formal constraints and informal constraints to characterize, respectively, the contractual and covenantal perspectives used in this anchoring point perspective on governance of corporations.

The difference between formal and informal constraints is one of degree. Sociologists and anthropologists envision a continuum from taboos, customs, and traditions at one end to written constitutions at the other.

The move, lengthy and uneven, from unwritten traditions and customs to written laws has been unidirectional in moving from less to more complex societies. The creation of formal legal systems to handle more complex disputes entails formal rules; hierarchies that evolve with more complex organizations entail formal structures to specify principal and agent relationships.

Formal rules include political (and judicial) rules and contracts. The hierarchy of such rules, from constitutions to statute and common laws to specific bylaws to individual contracts, defines constraints, from general rules to particular specifications. The function of formal rules is to promote certain kinds of exchange but not all exchange.

Formal rules in even the most developed economy make up a small, although very important, part of the sum of constraints that shape choice. It is readily apparent that informal constraints, or covenantal agreements (or disagreements), are more pervasive in the human interactions and relationships in families, external social relations, or in business activities where the governing structure is overwhelmingly defined by codes of conduct, attitudes, articles of faith, norms of behavior, and conventions.

Robert Axelrod provides a vivid illustration of a socially sanctioned norm of behavior. The night before he was to engage in a duel with Aaron Burr, Alexander Hamilton sat down and wrote out all the reasons why he should not accept this challenge. A crucial one, of course, was that he was likely to get killed. In spite of the overwhelming rational bases for not dueling, he felt that his effectiveness in the public arena would be significantly diminished by such a decision because dueling was the accepted way to settle disputes among gentlemen. Social norms dictated the choice, not formal rules.[2]

Professor North points out that we simply do not have any convincing theory of the sociology of knowledge that accounts for the effectiveness (or ineffectiveness) of organized ideologies or accounts for choices made when the payoffs to honesty, integrity, working hard, or voting are negative.[3]

Given this context, it is not surprising that we do not have a generally accepted theory of corporate governance. Obeying the unenforceable is too rich in variables for enterprise conduct and accountability to be modeled after informal constraints dealing with conventions requiring moral force.

STRATEGIC PROPRIETY

The logic and behavior of corporations affect other components of the overall political, economic, and social systems in which our free enterprise corporations operate. Actions draw on a complex repertoire of choices and relationships. These are available to individuals (directors) and organizations (boards) to employ in pursuit of their respective interests. This should occur while assuming the special characteristics and standards of what is socially acceptable in conduct.

Scholars of institutional theory view incorporation of an enterprise as the following: (1) a process of instilling value to the enterprise; (2) a creation of reality to a class of elements of the organization (i.e., marketing, financing, manufacturing); and (3) a complex of distinct societal spheres; a social creation in an economic, academic, political, military, or societal domain. A business enterprise is a social entity striving to exist in an economic environment.[4]

To further examine this notion of strategic propriety, the governance oversight and executive management of corporations has to be considered beyond its economic dimensions. Unfortunately, such social, ethical, political, or ecological relationships and consequences are not always well-managed components of strategic action unless required by law, as in the case of antitrust constraints.

Alexander Solzhenitsyn, speaking to the 1978 graduation class of Harvard College, said the following about legalistic relationships:

A society based on the letter of the law and never reaching any higher, fails to take advantage of the full range of human possibilities. The letter of the law is too cold and formal to have a beneficial influence on society. Whenever the tissue of life is woven of legalistic relationships, this creates an atmosphere of spiritual mediocrity that paralyzes men's noblest impulses. . . . After a certain level of the problem has been reached, legalistic thinking induces paralysis; it prevents one from seeing the scale and the meaning of events.[5]

PORTFOLIO PARTNERSHIP OF CONNECTIONS

The most common arrangement to bridge the divide between complex relationships is an adjusted association that clearly distinguishes between the separate streams of logic and proper behavior which flow to opposite sides of a corporate enterprise.

Lord Moulton's separate domains of Positive Law, Free Choice, and Manners, or obedience to the unenforceable, are foci for common understandings about what is appropriate and fundamentally meaningful behavior. This is a complex behavioral area studied by scholars in the field of social transactions and beyond the scope and focus of this book. An example is the tableau of how some directors proceed with the board meeting drill. They engage in a series of little standoffs and negotiated settlements of points lost or scored, confrontations met or evaded, bargains struck, and tensions or embarrassments accommodated. One study of the silent struggles of social interaction collected at least 1,000 specimens of embarrassment that were classified into seventy-four categories of *faux pas*, or gaffes. These were ultimately summarized into three clusters: (1) inappropriate identity, (2) loss of poise, and (3) disturbance of the assumptions persons make about one another in social transactions.[6]

Broadly speaking, however, there are two types of relationships in business and industry, contractual relationships and covenantal relationships.[7]

Contractual relationship covers the *quid pro quo* of working together. Three of the key elements in the art of working together are how to deal with change, how to deal with conflict, and how to reach our potential.

Covenantal relationships, on the other hand, induce freedom, not paralysis. A covenantal relationship rests on shared commitment to ideas, issues, goals, and management processes. Words such as empathy, warmth, and personal chemistry are certainly pertinent. They are open to influence. They fill deep needs and they enable work to have meaning and to be fulfilling.

Theologians point out the biblical idea of covenant as that which holds ethics together in concrete, historical experience. Covenant implies a bonded fidelity to responsive associations when they are formed under first principles of right and wrong and designed to serve those purposes that contribute to the ultimate and common good.

Covenantal relationships can reflect unity, grace, and poise. They are an expression of the sacred nature of relationships. They are based on personal trust, integrity, articles of faith, values, attitudes, morals, and ethics. Covenantal relationships enable corporations to be hospitable to the unusual person and unusual ideas. Covenantal relationships tolerate risks and forgive errors. Business philosopher Max Depree further believes that the best management process for today's environment is participative management based on covenantal relationships.

The role of the board and the individual director is to identify the contractual issues that are separate from the covenantal issues. Then, they can use informed judgment and make informed decisions.

It is perplexing that identifying and dealing with the covenantal issues involves both rational thought and emotions. The process is even more vexatious than coping with the complex principles of statutory and common law, the contractual side of the divide.

Your legal counsel will have *The Business Lawyer*, an August 1993 publication covering "The Symposium on Corporate Governance," which is pertinent to the challenge. This publication is the legal-regulatory perspective and is based on the American Law Institute (ALI) Project undertaken in 1978. This involved fifteen years of unremitting ALI debate about the scope and perimeter of the project.

The question asked was, "By what principles should incorporated enterprises be governed?" The product, this tome, has 822 densely printed pages and is two and one-half inches thick (paperbound).

GAMES DIRECTORS PLAY

Public faces behave differently in private places. Director faces are no exception, where covenantal relationships usually transcend contractual relationships.

The state of mind and the personality often shape the pattern of a director's covenantal behavior in the boardroom. This mind-set is sometimes wrapped up in individual ego states. The result is that directors often engage in ego games. These games are fascinating if you are aware of them. They usually occur only in the privacy of the boardroom. The games flush out personal beliefs, value systems, hidden agenda, emotional hang-ups, biases, human frailties, and political maneuverings.

One common thread in most directors' games is their well-defined, predictable outcomes despite any concealed motivations. Eric Berne called such transactions, "A series of moves with a snare." Also, the outcome usually has a dramatic quality about it. Histrionics accompanying a director's boardroom behavior often belie the ulterior nature of his or her position. The old maxim of raise your voice when your argument is weak, also holds in boardroom games.

An effective chairman will recognize the games underway and play along or redirect the psychodrama. This steering can be toward more rational reckoning and a realistic quality of the adult ego state of thinking and understanding. If the game is operating at the child's level of archaic fears or expectations or the parent level of a prim, righteous, prejudicial mindset cluttered with preconceived ideas, the adroit chairman can often nudge deliberations toward the adult state of conscious reasoning. Pulling off such a shift in group behavior is the hallmark of good chairmanship. It requires an understanding of personalities, a shrewd sense of timing, and insight into the ulterior quality of the posturing and rhetoric.

Ego games do not abide by the bylaws, the rituals, or the pastimes normally present in the board world. An ego game is never candid. It is essentially a series of superficially plausible moves with some concealed motive and a planned payoff. I include some disguised boardroom situations in which I have been involved in recent years where director ego states play ego games. The disguise is advisable, for the drama may be an inside story that should not be revealed to an outside director.

Five Covenantal Incidents

More often than not the sudden entry of the child comes as a shock when it happens on other occasions. It is not unusual for the child to pop up late in a board meeting when a particularly thorny problem surfaces requiring a lot of trade-offs of personal stakes or interests of individual directors, frequently in family dominated or closely held companies.

Incident One   The board of International Investments Ltd., pseudonym for a real company, had just decided to change its investment patterns in southern European countries. This meant partially abandoning the country where its founding had been, the little acorn from which had grown the great oak of the corporation.

It had been a painful discussion for all of the seven directors, four of whom were elder statesmen and immediate descendants of the founding families. The three younger directors, also related to the founding families though less directly, had attended graduate schools of business. An enlightened view of business strategy, the role of a board as distinct from management, and the issue of fiduciary responsibility of directors to all the shareowners had been inculcated in them. These matters troubled the younger members of the board. The issue before the board was a change in composition of membership through additional directors who would not be associated with the families holding sizable company ownership, although these families held only a small percentage of shares outstanding.

One of the more eloquent of the younger directors expounded at great length on the social consciousness and fiduciary accountability of the incumbent directors, seeing no need to perturb the closed circle of board membership with outsiders. He claimed they wouldn't fit the image of the corporation and its great heritage; the election of more directors would indicate that there was a failing on the part of the board. All sorts of subjective arguments for maintaining the status quo were emotionally presented.

What was really behind this impassioned performance was the child role at work: "How could I even explain this to my father, who had recently retired from the board at eighty years of age but whose influence still reigned?" Other members of the board in their adult states understood this. The chairman intervened and decided to delay any board changes until the time was more opportune and a more conscious reasoning would prevail.

Incident Two   Ego states were at play double-time in another board crisis when the newly elected chairman of Imeroil Ltd., again the pseudonym for a real company, was confronted by a challenge from one of his outside directors who sought to bully the newly elected chairman into deference and submission on financial policy matters in which the chairman was less experienced. The not-so-subtle contest over who had the best financial judgment took place over a nine-month period of stress. Arguments took place on both significant policy and procedural decisions concerning the financial strategy of the corporation, particularly in the area of foreign exchange risks.

At first, this was a covert test of wills. In some aspects, immature boardroom tactics and intuitive verbal fencing began to occur openly in board meetings as the bully and the chairman squared off repeatedly. The upshot was that the dissident director saw that his warfare was now in the open, and his struggle for power was attracting insufficient support from the other directors. He resigned because of what he called the press of other duties. The chairman had carefully played out this hidden power struggle in open board sessions in order to expose the lack of rapport. Without overtly stating that this was a conflict of wills, he let the challenger hang himself through the realization that if push came to shove on a board decision, the board would support the newly elected chairman, who at the time was also the CEO.

Looking back on this series of events and knowing the actors involved, I recall that the defecting director had always had his way during his successful business career. While his power tactics could be considered flowing in part from the child-ego state at work, he also superimposed some of the parent in borrowing preconceived ideas from his chairman-CEO role in his own company, where he ruled with an iron hand over a captive and docile board of directors. The bully role had child emotional content.

Incident Three   The international twist to the games directors play took place early in my association with the Transbay Corporation, another pseudonym, where I was privileged to work with the board of directors on the company's expansion into Latin America. The

American president of the company was a model of the ethical and professional marketing-type executive. He carried the corporate flag overseas with great aplomb. As was the custom, many of the trips abroad involved socializing with wives and families of overseas staffs, government officials, suppliers, customers, and financial executives. Transbay worked up a major investment project in the $36 million range for a Brazilian factory near Campinas. The economic evaluation, the country's risk assessment, and other elements of the project were favorable, and the project was up for consideration by the full board. The president had warmed up the outside directors for over a year while the engineering and marketing work was done to support the appropriation request.

The top management and the four inside members of the board had labored hard to support their chief's presentation. At the last minute, the proposal was stricken from the board's agenda and the president explained to his board that he and management had had second thoughts about the political stability of Brazil in the years ahead and therefore were deferring any further action. I later found out that his turning point in advocacy was triggered by and coincided with the president's trip to Sao Paulo about six weeks before the board meeting to check again on the local situation. His wife had been pinched on the Corcovado, or better said, she was pinched when they stopped off en route to Rio de Janeiro and took the aerial tram to the top of Hunchback Mountain.

The parent-ego prejudice against foreigners was bruised when the primly righteous lady was admired and tweaked from behind by a Brazilian national. Apparently this was not the place the respectable Transbay Corporation should carry on its business, according to the president's reactive interpretation. The parent in his spouse (perhaps her archaic child fears lay at the bottom?) suppressed the adult in the president. The board never knew the real reasons for management's change of attitude, and Brazil lost a major international investor. On the other hand, the company lost an opportunity to place its manufacturing in a growing, if somewhat risky, market. The company never recovered its enthusiasm for Brazil and still has not made a serious commitment there.

Incident Four In upper New York State, I was attending a board meeting where the president, newly appointed following an outside search, was in high-gear discussion with his directors. Having been sought after and lured away from another chief executive position, he was feeling his oats, and his manner was that of a lecturer to freshman students. The parent mind-set was obvious in his preconceived ideas borrowed from his previous career. Over a period of several meetings he dealt with the board members in a condescending way as if they were in the child state of mind.

The nonexecutive chairman was an understanding, wise old hand with the company and had been instrumental in getting the new CEO aboard. The outside board members were also quite adult in their personalities and understandings. They were attuned to the realities of the developing situation. The company was in dire need of firm, professional leadership. But the cocky, new CEO went too far in imposing his parental ego on the board at a meeting where forward strategy was debated. He became so adamant about his ideas that the chairman, sensing a near blowup, called for a recess. He took the CEO by the hand, walked him to a nearby lakeshore, and assumed the parent role long enough to tell the CEO he would have to accede to the board's position. Otherwise, the outside directors would resign or replace him.

This obviously rattled the CEO, and to his credit he moved his mental set one notch forward, where rational reckoning and logical decision making took over, and, above all, he accepted the reality of his position and tactics.

A kind and shrewd chairman can intervene effectively when director transaction states are in conflict or not congruent.

Incident Five   A most colorful director drama took place in South America six years ago. All three personality structures were in action amid the boardroom ceremonials that Latin cultures offer with such *elegancia*. The child, the parent, and the adult competed for airtime in this boardroom story, both in the actions and in the pantomime involved.

I was consulting for the chairman of a quasi-government–owned, Latin American–based corporation. My colleagues had briefed me on the politically sensitive board situation that had resulted primarily from the character of the large natural resource-oriented company. But I was unprepared for the board play and gaming that was to come.

My task was to outline a new role for the directors. This addressed the conventional governance problems inherent in their multiproduct, far-flung national enterprise that afforded employment to a great many citizens of this benevolently led nation.

I was ushered into a dimly lit, mahogany-paneled boardroom and seated at the head of the twenty-five-foot-long jacaranda table. Eight board members were seated at the table, which had a microphone in front of each director. A battery of an *ayudante de campo*, two translators, and three stenographers were positioned in seats against the walls. On my right was the bilingual, well-groomed chairman, the friendliest person in the room. On my left were two appropriately clad union representatives. There were five other men: a conservative-looking professor, two formally dressed executives of the company, a uniformed deputy minister of defense, and the fifth, who outshone us all. He was an air force general, right out of the movie stereotype. His uniform was magnificent, his hair and manner were De Lorean, and his display of medals was enormous.

My tutorial was translated loudly and simultaneously from the sidelines; the mikes were superfluous. My English-language presentation on the contrapuntal effect of the governance truths about conflicts of interest, insider's dealings, social responsibility, and fiduciary duties, pitched against the mellifluous Spanish version, made the session an unusually confusing one.

When I had finished, the game playing began. The union leaders brought forth the child personality as they defended their constituents' point of view, dominated by a natural fear of any change and unrealistic expectations as to future gains for their members. The parent personality was clearly evident in the posturing of the government representatives, who were thinking about how difficult it would be to present any change to the political leaders who had appointed them to monitor (not change) the corporation. The adult game was skillfully played by the chairman, who marshaled the conversations and processed them gracefully to get members of the board to see the realistic need for change. It was masterful chairing of a crossfire of transactions between directors as they politely debated. The proposed change in the role of the board meant abandoning the past practice of overcontrol and stalemate on any issue that impinged on historical entitlements of the constituents, particularly workers' benefits and the vested interests of certain directors.

I learned more about the game playing in a later, private session with the chairman. He indicated that the board had recorded the session and played the tapes for the executive committee of the board, which sorted out the issues and policy choices that were obscured by the games played on the day of my presentation.

Directors do behave differently from what one might expect in the privacy of the boardroom. That's part of the mystique that shrouds boardrooms. The criteria and standards for boardworthiness are elusive, ineffable, subjective, or defiant of reason. The games directors play need to be recognized in this setting in order to understand how boards of directors actually carry out their functions.

This game playing is why a closed door is essential despite the activists' cry for "sunshine in the boardroom," or more public disclosure of board affairs. The in camera nature of board deliberations obscures most of the petty faults and anachronisms and allows interpersonal, covenantal relationships of directors to incubate and manifest their respective levels of ego states. Trade-offs are made amid the rivalries of competing uncertain perspectives and interests. Conflict, tension, pacification, cooperations, coaptation, persuasion, bargaining, and maneuvering are involved in the games that directors play.

Adult chairmanship can referee these games and tactics to make a board more effective. Corporate counsel and certified public accountants advise on and can monitor the contractual relationships of directors and executive management.

THE CEO'S ROLE IN BUILDING RELATIONSHIPS WITH THE BOARD[8]

It is not enough just to select the proper board. Indeed, with the people in place, the process of CEO-director interaction has barely begun. Not until the CEO begins to use the talents, skills, and diverse energies of board members to best advantage is the full power of the relationship realized. The resources available to the CEO and directors help him or her to shape the power partnership between board and company management.

Boards vary as to relationships between management and the directors. Entrepreneurial companies prize patience in their directors. Older, closely held family businesses may require directors who acknowledge that the board isn't democratic; the head of the family or head of the board is more equal than the rest of the directors combined. Companies with a public trust need a CEO who not only tolerates but encourages the kind of board initiative that a variety of opinions provides.

Building a power partnership may be easier in a "double C" situation—one in which chairman and CEO are one person. Exercising control and power becomes simpler. Many CEOs resist separating these roles so they won't have to develop relationships with both the directors and a separate nonexecutive chairman. The rationale for separating the chairman and CEO roles is based on the notion of separation of CEO power from board power. This need varies depending on the maturity of the CEO-board relationship, its patterns of interaction, the nature and ownership of the enterprise, and its size and competitive position. The goal is an effective balance of the latent power of the board and the kinetic power of the CEO.

Three models describe the most common CEO/board configurations. There is the ideal model which is a situation that calls for directors to tend to the governance of the company, with minimal involvement in day-to-day operations. This assumes an effective CEO and a healthy relationship with the board. Less ideal are the two other models. These vary as to which are less than ideal, how much attention a director member pays to the board process, how involved he becomes in the company, and the leadership role and performance of the CEO and the enterprise.

In building the partnership, the wise CEO identifies the proper balance of interests. If he or she finds that ideal balance in the board, the CEO uses its strength to continually reinforce the effectiveness of both the board and the institution it serves. When that ideal is absent, the CEO studies the strengths, weaknesses, and interests of each director to determine who adds value and who detracts. Once the CEO has completed this process of identification, he or she can get on with the task of building the partnership.

Nose In, Fingers Out (NIFO)

The NIFO scheme of director participation works well in almost any corporate environment and is the model most CEOs would prefer. Its statement is a succinct caution to independent, outside directors: Concentrate on overseeing and monitoring management's performance, and then get the hell out of the way. At the same time, the board remains readily available as a resource to the CEO when he or she needs help.

Nose In, Fingers In (NIFI)

Yes, it is possible for a director to care too much, to be too involved, and to be too nosy. Even the most objective outside director finds it difficult to take both macro and micro approaches to be able to have perspective on the big picture and still worry about each brush stroke of management.

There's a certain degree of common sense in including a few active executives on a board. Such participants can ground discussions in reality, keep the focus on pragmatic issues, and define both what's possible and what's not. But the NIFI management director should be recognized for his greatest strength: The ability to bring an insider's perspective and have the wherewithal to help educate outsiders.

This function of an inside director often manifests itself in an adjunct advisory committee or council rather than in a statutory board membership. Whatever the case, as long as there is a healthy balance of NIFO directors outweighing the NIFI exceptions, the CEO can maintain the equilibrium he or she needs to sustain the partnership of power with the appropriate degrees of kinetic and latent action or oversight.

Nose Out, Fingers Out (NOFO)

There are two kinds of indirect harm generated by the NOFO director: (1) He is filling a seat that could be taken by someone who could contribute to the board and the company's well being; and (2) there's always the possibility that his ennui will become contagious and that his peers will get the idea that directorship is a passive honorary position. With the current public spotlight on ineffective boards, this is an anachronistic role.

NOFOs are often some of your oldest associates—people who have been with your board for so long that you might not notice their passivity. But there are always hints. "Where's the annual general meeting dinner this year, Bob," he'll ask. Or the suggestions he offers about management begin to take a selfish edge. For example, "How about a meeting down South?" is a cue that there's a problem. He continues, "Couple of days in the sunshine, a few rounds of golf?"

It is the NOFO no-win situation that a CEO should confront head on. The bipolar association between the board and the CEO purposely creates a set of checks and balances that benefits shareholders. The power partnership between CEO and board works best when the independence is equal, the dependance mutual, and the obligations reciprocal. There is no place for a completely arm's-length directorship.

Tom Tyler, former president of Shuttleworth Inc., in Huntington, Indiana, came to his position in 1980. He knew the company well in that he had spent six months as one of its few outside directors. His challenge as a nonfamily, implanted executive was to help a family start-up that was having trouble growing beyond its entrepreneurial roots. To do so, he had to find a board receptive to change from a passive posture to a more active involvement.

"When I came into the company, the Shuttleworth family and I sat down and talked about what the board should be," Tyler recalls. "We wanted skills. We didn't want shareholders."

Shuttleworth manufactures automation systems (known as conveyor belts) that the company sells to a number of firms worldwide that have specialized needs for packaging, printing, binding, and electronics assembly. When Tyler joined the company as chief operating officer, he arrived with a background in engineering, finance, sales, international management, and marketing. He was already a member of the company's five-person board, a group that also included the president, the president's wife, and two minority shareholders whose principal interest was in getting some sort of return on their investment.

The new board Tyler assembled included the two original outsiders, a financier and a local community leader. They had been NIFI directors, too concerned about the company's financial performance and too preoccupied with the return on their investment. But Tyler sensed that they had been around long enough to understand the company's long-term strengths and weaknesses. It was knowledge and experience that Tyler wanted on his board and he would not be able to find these elsewhere.

To eliminate any conflict of interest, he convinced the Shuttleworth family to buy out the minority investors' interest. Then he paid the two a fee to continue as board members. "They felt properly rewarded for their skills," Tyler says, "and they loved the company.

They were part of its history, part of its growing up. We bought them out, they probably made a 100-percent capital gain on their investment, and they liked the way we were treating them as professional board members."

Tyler had his first NIFO directors. To further build his partnership with the board, he added a professional marketing executive, an attorney, and a local businessman.

"The board understands that the Shuttleworth family represents the total shareholders, the only ones with anything at risk," Tyler explains. "But the family is smart enough to want an honest opinion from the board. As a result, there can be some controversy during our meetings, but it is limited to the kind of discussion that comes from a director in an adviser's capacity.

"We don't see outside directors taking a hard position. The Shuttleworths are wise enough to keep an open mind and listen. But the family members have a hard sense of position. If the Shuttleworths and I agree on a certain posture, we make our recommendations clear before the board sits. After the meeting, we then review what we've heard from the outside directors. The directors become, in effect, a sounding board. A resource."

The synergy between this implanted chief operating officer, the Shuttleworth family, and the outside board is exemplary. But it is not easy to find. Tyler advises, "Although these roles are constantly changing, there is that magic word, communication, that has to be a part of the formula. If you can share beliefs and ideas but don't communicate them to each other, you might not know that you have that ground in common.

"The CEO," Tyler continues, has a clear mandate of building "a sense of trust and belief in one another, so you can say anything you wish. That is a blessing in my situation because I know I can say whatever I wish and know that even if the Shuttleworths don't agree, if nothing else, they will listen and give me an honest answer."

The NIFO board's effectiveness is proof of the pudding. "We don't mask anything," Tom Tyler concludes. "Seventy percent of our time with the directors is spent on education. Thirty percent is invested in asking them for input on the information we've passed on to them. I've been on the board of directors for more than ten years and there has never been a major decision that has been anything but unanimous."

During that period, Shuttleworth unquestionably grew from a company floundering in financial insecurity to one with multinational operations—a joint venture in Japan, a wholly owned European subsidiary, and a board of directors wise enough to keep its nose in but its fingers out.

When the trusteeship of a company spreads beyond its originating founders and managers, the power relationships will inevitably become more complicated. But as long as the CEO manages these complications, understanding the potential of a balanced partnership, they do not have to translate directly into problems.

A PERSONAL CASE STUDY ON BUILDING RELATIONSHIPS WITH THE BOARD

In 1952, I became president/CEO and a director of a daughter company created by Monsanto and Shawinigan Chemical Company (SCC) headquartered in Shawinigan Falls, Quebec. Shawinigan Resins Corporation (SRC), as the joint venture was called, was based adjacent to our Monsanto operations in Indian Orchard, Massachusetts. It marked my first industrial boardroom experience and my first challenge in building partnership with a board to enhance company performance.

The company was put together to develop, manufacture, and market a new resin interlayer that replaced the acetate interlayer in safety-glass windshields. Because Monsanto had been successful in producing and selling the earlier safety-glass laminate interlayer, it had the plant, distribution, marketing, and sales networks in place. Shawinigan Chemical had the patents for the resin compound. We needed that technology to move to the next stage of growth, so our alignment was a natural one.

SRC's board consisted strictly of insiders from the parent corporation's owners, and it was their mandate to oversee the new company's development and ensure the effectiveness of the key management group. Whenever there was confusion between the two principal parties, the inevitable result was a bargaining session between me, the American SRC chairman, and my Canadian SCC chairman counterpart. Whatever we decided went into effect, ratified by the daughter board made up of captive directors from each of the joint-venture companies.

It all seemed so simple, so logical. Our board left us alone to do our business. It was a rubber-stamp NOFO group that supported us without questioning our every decision. On paper, it looked great.

We did not fully appreciate how difficult and time consuming it would be to scale up the manufacturing process and work out the technical bugs for full-scale production. Long before we were able to devote any energy to a long-term strategic business plan, we had to resolve our production problems, difficulties that were compounded by pricing considerations. As competition developed, we were tied into paying a higher price for raw materials because of our original sole-source supply arrangement with our Canadian partner. So much for the plan on paper.

Our partner was sometimes troublesome in matters that extended far beyond simple dollars-and-cents considerations. Let me introduce you to one of the Canadian SRC consultants. He was a long-dead, roly-poly, Zero Mostel look-alike whose mystique stemmed from his role as Shawinigan Chemical's scientific guru. He was an inventor and insisted that we consult him on every technical decision, a position fully backed by my Canadian counterpart and his captive board members in our joint venture. There was no question that back in St. Louis, Monsanto had more talent than our research group could ever draw on. But the Canadians deferred to this individual. And as long as they had equal board votes to force any issue, we deferred.

While the good doctor was just plain strange, our partners also found a way to include the outright eccentric in their management program. Specifically, I speak of a Britisher who had come to Canada with a number of ideas and had actually patented a few for Shawinigan Chemical. Because our manufacturing plant was in Springfield, he often would accompany the Canadian directors for an inspection of our facilities after the board meetings. Seemingly innocent, his presence was notable in that he showed up in a safari outfit; no pith helmet, but a complete South African outfit of shorts and a khaki, short-sleeved shirt.

While he was usually charming in his dealings with coworkers, there was one occasion when he became a problem. A piece of extrusion equipment blew during his tour and sprayed formic acid (the pain inducer in beestings) on his legs. Had he been dressed like everyone else in the plant, he would have been protected. But garbed only in safety glasses and his safari togs, he was burned.

The injury was not as serious as it could have been—he was only hit in the knees—but the event was more emblematic than real because we had to decide who was wearing the pants in this joint relationship. In particular, we had to find a way to turn this joint-venture relationship into a professional NIFO directorate and to move SRC away from the schizophrenia generated by its split parentage.

There was only so much we could do. Many of the duties and responsibilities of the board were prescribed by the bylaws and the contract between the two owners. Continuing to head up Monsanto's Springfield-based headquarters for worldwide plastics operations, I also took on the chairmanship of the joint venture.

During the eleven years spent concerned with the fortunes of SRC, I learned several lessons. I discovered that any time things seemed to be working smoothly, it was probably because we didn't have the information about the things that were quietly going wrong. I found that a board of insiders could do a terrific job of recognizing individual performance but had a far more difficult time assigning individual responsibility. I learned that strategies develop most easily from backlogs, that our company's share of market most often was smaller than we thought, and that the number of competitors never declines. And, in direct reference to board membership, I came to believe that only mediocre directors are always at their best and that, if you have been to enough board meetings over a long period of time, the meetings themselves often become more important than the issues.

It is ultimately the CEO's job to build the partnership, and it was ultimately my job to turn the NOFO board of approval into a NIFO board of directors. Instead of nodding heads, we found a diverse group of knowledgeable people who were able to point us in the right direction. We began to work our way out of our tribulations only as we began to identify the issues of control and act on them responsibly. The key to our successful business was a clear understanding of the roles of the CEO, the chairman, and the board, as well as of their respective powers at different stages of the company's development.

The final answer for SRC was a Dutch auction. Monsanto offered a price for Shawinigan Chemical's interest and the option for our partners to match the offer and take over the entire operation. Our Canadian colleagues declined, and we consolidated the entire operation under the direction of Monsanto.

I came away from the experience with a changed perspective on how critical the CEO is to building a power partnership with his or her board. It was much the same message that Tom Tyler found out in Huntington, Indiana: The balance of power and the long-term success of a company largely depend on a board independent enough to counsel, a chairman smart enough to listen, and a president strong enough to act.

MATCHING DIRECTORS WITH THEIR BOARDS, OR PICKING YOUR PARENTS

Board member selection is one of a CEO's most important concerns and certainly one of the oddest. The power of choice rightly rests with a more independent authority: a nominating committee that is usually dominated by outside directors. But the intelligent CEO realizes that his or her powers of suggestion still carry weight, so the CEO searches for the right kind of candidate, too. The quest demands all the skill brought to bear in a courtship. The process even suggests the romance of a marriage. But as a CEO romances his or her candidate, pragmatism necessarily tempers a relationship that is grounded in strictly business affairs. In assembling a board, the CEO has to keep in mind the strong family, or tribal, component that should support the CEO/board relationship. For the CEO, relationship with the board is really not so much one of marriage as it is of parentage. Ideally, a CEO's board members become his bosses and, in effect, his parents. It is an oddly balanced kind of partnership in that one collective party has the authority to fire the other. That's a tough way to embark on any kind of marriage. As long as we live in a society that prefers one spouse at a time, the model is even more awkward.

When a CEO becomes overly involved in the nomination process of board members, it is akin to picking parents as far as he or she is concerned. While the CEO cannot legally control the election of a board without having a controlling interest, that individual is always slightly more equal in the relationship. What the CEO should look for as he or she inherits directors is a group of people who will provide the kind of support, counsel, and oversight needed. Ideally, it becomes a full family—a number of individuals who bring a variety of skills and strengths to a corporation as active, concerned, and intelligent contributors to overseeing and governing the enterprise.

In the mid-1970s, a group in the executive development unit at the London Business School conducted some research on matching directors with their boards. Their studies led to four models—relationships that matched the ways families adjust to day-to-day married life with the ways in which CEOs match up in different board partnerships.[9]

Portfolio Partnership The most common arrangement, the portfolio partnership, is an adjusted association that clearly distinguishes between the separate roles of the CEO and board. The CEO takes charge and is responsible to the board for leading the enterprise. The board is accountable to the owners for selecting the CEO, supporting or replacing the CEO, and for the general oversight of corporate affairs.

Intertwining Partnership This is the second most common pattern and consists of two involved parties working together (intertwining) on fiduciary accountabilities, strategic direction, and corporate leadership.

Competitive Partnership In this model, the board members and the CEO are all successful business people familiar with the company they serve. The relationship is one of friendly professional rivalry with the two parties working together primarily to benefit the company and its shareholders. In this instance, however, the directors have separate outside accountabilities.

Self-Sufficient Partnership The CEO and the board have completely separate existences and accommodate each other only when both parties' responsibilities are in question. In this model, the two parties are less attuned to each other's values and attitudes than in the other three. They pay little attention to how the media, the local community, government regulators, or the public see the company.

What model suits what kind of company? That is largely the chairman's decision. But whatever choice he follows, the chairman must take full responsibility for it. The chairman and the CEO must recognize changing patterns and discern when an adjustment in the business or the business environment calls for a concomitant adjustment in the partnership. Otherwise, the CEO/board relationship may be endangered. Portfolio thinking and communication are both essential features of the partnership.

David L. Coffin, chairman of the oldest firm on the New York Stock Exchange, gives some succinct advice on the subject of selecting board parentage. He says, "They're easier to get than to unget."

That's the bad news. Ensuring the good news, he says, starts with the right balance and, contrary to what one might think, diversity of people. He says, "I've always taken a hard line on outside board members. I believe that outside board members are people you cannot afford to hire because if you could afford to hire them, you would. And then you would talk to them twenty-four hours a day."

Coffin is the former chairman and CEO of the Dexter Corporation in Windsor Locks, Connecticut. This international manufacturer of specialty chemicals and materials was founded in 1767, when half its ledger was in pounds sterling and half in American dollars.

Coffin replaced his father as president of the family-controlled $850-million business in 1958 and stayed on in the job until 1990, when he became nonexecutive chairman. In a family business, there is always the option of maintaining tight control and packing the board with cronies. But when it came his turn to take over the business and participate in picking his own business parents, David Coffin weighed in on the side of diversity.

Coffin emphasizes, "Hiring outsiders diversifies the board with the talent you need—technology, education, management expertise, marketing." In thirty-two years as the president of Dexter Corporation, Coffin specifically sought out chief executives because he felt they understood the need to be "more than just one-day-a-quarter people. They were to be partners you could call on anytime, day or night." Three of the company's eleven current directors have CEO experience in other industries. Both the weight of the office and the passage of time have taught them a vital virtue: patience. As Coffin watched Dexter's needs start to change, he sought to adjust his board. Because the U.S. consciousness was beginning to focus on the European marketplace, he signed on the retired head of environmental management for the country of France. "First-class," Coffin says. "He wanted to learn more about American industry and is using Dexter for that education. We have enough assets in Europe that we needed his type of experience and counsel. Now we want to put in someone with Asian experience as we look to those markets for growth."

Moving too far afield from familiar territory, Coffin allows, can be troublesome. "I remember, years ago, that you usually invited someone onto your board whom you already knew. 'I've known this person for ten years,' you say to yourself, 'and my father knew him before that. He'll make a good board member. He's respected in the community. Everybody likes him.' Now you get a headhunter and say, 'Here's fifteen thousand bucks. Get me a board member. Here's a profile. I want this kind of guy.' All of a sudden, you get ten resumes on your desk with pictures and press clippings, and the headhunter says any one of them is exactly what you need. Now where are you? You have a much more difficult situation than you would have had with the good ol' boy."

Ideally, board members are heroic; they bring courage, bold enterprise, intellectual power, and nobility of purpose to their work. They are leaders who uplift ambitions, who apply a higher standard of performance to almost any task, and whose very presence makes everyone work harder and smarter. On occasion, they come out of the old-boy system. I met my first two heroes at the first board meeting I ever attended.

In 1938, I had been working for Monsanto in St. Louis, supervising some chemical-plant operators, when I joined a group of middle managers overseeing the company's Indian Orchard plant in Springfield, Massachusetts. It was a fast track for a young man just three years out of graduate school, and those of us assigned to the project were lucky enough to have a reasonable goal: assist in Monsanto's absorption of a newly acquired company that made billiard-ball-type plastic and needed to be brought into the twentieth century.

Edgar Monsanto Queeny, hero number one, was the man in charge of the company that had been started by his father in 1904. Edgar was a modest, retiring person. Not a great speaker, he preferred listening and quiet thought to talking and haphazard action. He was smart enough to recruit managers who were not just capable but were role models for the next generation of employees.

Queeny was also wise enough to sense that he needed something extra for his board and he diverged from the comfortable industry choices whenever he had a chance to add to the assembly that governed company coffers. In 1945, our group petitioned this board for a $500,000 appropriation to build a new polymerization plant in Springfield. By that time, I was vice president and general manager of the company's plastic division, including the Indian Orchard operation. An aggressive ensemble, we always assumed a fiercely combative posture toward our competition. We rehearsed our board presentation just as a general's staff would prime for a battle. We had market surveys. We had projections. We had graphs, charts, and flip charts. We were prepared for a preemptive strike that would win our division glory and honor. If asked, "What are you going to do?" we were ready with the answers. If asked, "When are you going to do it?" we had the response prepared. If asked, "Why do we need this now?" our reply was that there was no one in the plastics business who knew better than we did.

A written request had gone through the internal management hierarchy. The one question we couldn't answer, "How are you going to finance it?" was the only query we would leave to the expertise of Queeny's Monsanto board.

In my presentation to that group, I highlighted the project's virtues, our proprietary technology, the product's potential market acceptance, and our plans to control the hazardous aspects of the operation. I presented our production-cost estimates to the second decimal place and projected return on investment far beyond the company norm.

As the presentation continued, the spotlight shifted to our internal capabilities, our confidence in the merits of the project, and our ability to recoup the investment in a few years. I let the board know that we had both the skilled operators and the management talent it would take to complete the project on time. There was no question that we could sell whatever we produced. I asked the board for approval.

There was silence, interrupted only when one of the outside directors leaned over to Queeny and whispered something in his ear. Queeny nodded, jotted down some notes, looked up at me, and said, "We like the idea." I breathed a sigh of relief.

Queeny didn't miss a beat as he continued. "When would you be able to go beyond your original proposal and install two more units in Springfield and place self-contained plants in Mexico, Argentina, and Britain?"

I was no longer relieved. I was stunned. More to the point, I was stumped. I had answers to all the short-term questions but none of us at Indian Orchard had given proper consideration to long-term global prospects for the new process. We had prepared for an approval for one Springfield unit. But we had no answer for two additional home-base installations. And the thought of facilities in Mexico, Argentina, and Britain had never crossed our minds. Queeny had been prodded by Charles S. Cheston, an investment banker at Smith, Barney & Co.'s Philadelphia office and the second hero I encountered at that first board meeting I ever attended.

Edgar Queeny knew his business and Monsanto's potential. But Charlie Cheston knew international finance. The two men were more than just codirectors, they were great friends. While that personal association made the meetings all the more pleasant, it never compromised the business at hand. In no way would Cheston upstage his chairman, a mistake less sophisticated directors would make in those days and still do make some fifty years later. Everyone in that room knew that Edgar had the final say on everything, even though he never said very much, but he was wise enough to welcome the advice of people who knew more than he.

When Charlie Cheston leaned over to Edgar Queeny and said, "Let's go," it was a heroic act that demonstrated just how smart the Monsanto chair had been in picking his parents. A young executive was making his first appearance before the board to advocate a new installation in Springfield. Cheston had the vision to see the full potential of financing the project. And Queeny had the intelligence to act on his colleague's counsel.

The same scenario would never unfold with that kind of dispatch today. Fifty years ago, however, it was not unusual to have your banker and your lawyer on your board. When the alliance worked, it worked well. But the government has since recognized the conflict-of-interest potential of allowing outside people who are paid to provide a service to the company with a service to perform as board members also. While sage friends and counselors such as Charlie Cheston can and should be advisers, most companies try to avoid any perception of conflict by keeping such outside contractors away from the formal decision making and fiduciary roles of the board.

The rules have changed. Pressure from both major investors and the Securities and Exchange Commission (SEC) has encouraged the use of outside-director-dominated nominating committees. But some of the fundamental principles of board selection, namely, picking the right kinds of board members for parental oversight and direction, still apply. The judicious selectors continue to seek out directors who will strengthen the partnership concept.

To encourage change and to anticipate shifts in market conditions, the sage CEO looks for differences in background, value systems, and attitudes for board membership. The unquestioning comfort of the small start-up is sacrificed for the commonsense and fiduciary duty of directors who have the depth to call attention to what-if situations.

The most sophisticated boards today operate more effectively with a predominance of outside independent directors. A board meeting may last only two to three hours with as few as four to six sessions a year. It can often be a showcase for young executives with expansive ideas and proposals that need the polish that comes from different kinds of expertise and the courage generated by experience.

In picking your heroes, look for your Charlie Chestons and Edgar Queenys. Seek intelligence. Complement your own wisdom. Be prepared to manage contentiousness but be wary of complacency. Look for people who are willing not just to lead but to inspire, whose very association with the present generation of management inspires the next group of leaders. These are truly business heroes whose willingness to boldly act can provide a legacy of boardroom excellence. Bring in people that you can't afford to hire. Listen to them. Act on their counsel. As company needs evolve, don't hesitate to reconstruct your board to better meet new demands. Follow the examples of Coffin and Queeny in your quest for appropriate parentage by way of a more resourceful board, a more effective chairman, and a more successful company.

5

Power in Pinstripes: Partnership of CEO and the Board

The power partnership between the CEO and the board of directors is the fulcrum, or the support point, that allows the CEO and the directors to strike a dynamic balance of power. It is the point where the controlling interests or their surrogates work to form a complementary, pivotal partnership with those in pinstripes. This coupled arrangement lets an enterprise do its best work.

In reviewing a recent book related to this subject, the pinstripe profile was so dubbed by Alex Lajoux, director of NACD Publications and Research of *Directors Monthly*, a publication of the National Association of Corporate Directors.

This archetype of those in power positions sometimes depicts a troublesome tableau of use, abuse, retention, and delegation of power, both contractual and covenantal. The trend in a number of boardrooms worldwide can become a serious dysfunction in both for-profit and nonprofit domains. In the great majority of corporations, however, the tableau exists as a chronic challenge to governance and management. In recent years, too many acute abuse events have metastasized into boardroom scandals where there was outright disobedience to the unenforceable.

The target model for the balanced power partnership has certain characteristics. Independence is equal. Dependence is mutual. Obligations are reciprocal. Through cooperation and collaboration, the CEO and the board balance their overlapping roles, their accountabilities, and their powers. Above all, they obey the unenforceable, covenantal relationships required for effective governance and executive management.

THE CONTROLLING INTEREST

To a large degree, success is attributable to human factors. While it is true that the basic legal accountability of the board is to insure that an enterprise is governed and managed in the best interests of its stockholders, that mandate is only the beginning. And while the CEO operates with the elected support of a board that assigns him or her the authority, that charter is only as effective as the people who manage both ends of it.

To understand control, we must move beyond legal definitions into the human condition. An enterprise exists in elevators, in boardrooms, in strategic planning sessions away from the office, in shared vision, and in the knowledge of one individual complementing the wisdom of another. Aligning the powers of the board with the powers it cedes to the CEO is a human balancing act in that it involves an artful alliance—a team becomes stronger only as all the different players bring their different talents to the table.

The controlling issue is a people issue. The right people who bring the right mix of talents and strengths are more important to a company than the right legal carapace. Carefully selected parents can govern a badly constructed corporate shell. On the other hand, ineffective directors are a detriment to even the most thoughtfully conceived company.

The contract that matters most in the relationship between a chief executive and a board is the one-on-one social contract of mutual respect between each director and the CEO. It is a matter of dual competency. The board's ability to govern is coupled with the CEO's ability to manage the company's activities.

When either party dominates, the red flags of warning become immediately evident. An unbalanced partnership may not only eliminate the effectiveness of the checks-and-balances strength of the board but may also cripple the executive's leadership capability. When the directors and the CEO compete rather than collaborate, the balance of the seesaw is tipped and the partnership is damaged.

The relationship is based on mutual respect and trust. This basis is paradoxical in that the board elects and employs the CEO, yet most directors acknowledge the chief executive as the enterprise's (and often the board's) *de facto* leader. The relationship is also based on exchange, wherein the two parties rely on each other to furnish information, credibility, and support. With that exchange, each performs more effectively.

To paraphrase D. H. Lawrence's vision of marriage, the power partnership of the CEO and the board of directors is the great business puzzle of the next decade. Understand it or be blown to bits by your ignorance. This is the central message.

Because we are dealing with issues that fall into areas of social science and behavior, there is no general maxim we can rely on to point us toward the perfect partnership. There are only models, and there are as many models as there are different types of corporations. The closely held family business demands which kind of partnership is used. An entrepreneurial venture on a growth-through-acquisition binge mandates another kind of model. A fully mature multinational manufacturer requires yet another model.

The more examples we cite, the closer we are to constructing a model with universal applicability. There will always be exceptions to whatever rules we create as long as the balance—the controlling issue—is strongly tied to people.

William M. Crozier, Jr., explains the power balance relationship in mechanical terms. "It's something like the function gasoline provides for an engine. The engine can't work without gasoline. And the gasoline is nothing unless it has an engine to work in. The gasoline is the chief executive; the board is the engine. They both function for a purpose, but they only function together."

Crozier is chairman and CEO of BayBanks Inc., a Boston-based commercial bank holding company with $9.9 billion in assets. He concedes that his example has the same problem as the mechanical model in that there are an almost infinite number of engine types and a wide variety of fuels. As "an airplane engine is different from a lawn mower engine," so any particular company has specific needs for a board and a CEO that are unlike any other.

The engine Bill Crozier joined in 1974 was badly in need of repair. He was perceived as a high-octane savior who would come to the rescue of BayBanks's unhappy board, its restless senior management, its disconsolate chairman, and a number of downright angry operating executives in subsidiary functions.

Crozier went right to work to find the proper power balance with his board—a group of people already in place who, by and large, were several years his senior. "I had the choice of totally ignoring them or of benefiting from their experience and their wisdom." With unrest throughout the company, Crozier confesses that he found the situation "scary, because, all of a sudden, you can find yourself in a potentially uncontrollable situation." He explains:

When you ask people's opinions, you don't always get confirmation of what seems right to you. You get a whole universe of thought—you learn reality, and that's scary—knowing the risks. But that's why you do it.

As you learn what the parameters are, it is both reassuring and scary at the same time. It is reassuring to know about the variety of opinion that exists, as opposed to not knowing about it at all. You think you know what you're up against when you become CEO, but as you learn what you're really up against, it becomes your job to overcome the challenges. You real- ize that your career is on the line and you see what you, personally, have at risk. That gets scarier as you approach the finish line.

The quest for corporate knowledge was not an easy adventure for Crozier when he first came to BayBanks. "It is a very difficult thing for a younger executive to imagine he doesn't have the prin- cipal power," he recalls. "I think that is an issue of inexperience as much as anything else. It has to do with personalities."

To demonstrate the frustration of newly acquired power, Crozier steps away from the corporate realm to the very private inside busi- ness of one of Boston's most venerable social clubs. He continues,

The board of governors was in trouble, after many years of neglect—the club was threadbare and loving it; the food quality was going down and every- thing else seemed to follow. When it finally hit bottom, they hired a new manager—a young man full of energy, full of ideas. "You fix it," they tell him. But he starts to do his job and they scream, "You're making all the employ- ees unhappy. This is an unhappy situation. Your plan is not working."

In other words, if people want a strong CEO to "fix things," they can't grab him around the collar every five minutes and say, "Now, you shouldn't do this, and you should do that." If they do, the CEO will shrivel up and quit.

If, in its consummate wisdom, your board has properly selected the per- son who is going to lead the company out of some sort of corporate morass, it should transfer enough power to let him do the job. That transfer—whether it's at the oh-so-proper Boston club or in the less-than-perfect business world—is the issue that creates either power conflict or power partnership.

When Bill Crozier came to BayBanks, he embraced the power of control at the same time that he sought his board's assistance in bringing receptive power to the company. "In the ideal case for a CEO," he says, "if you have youthful energy, you want to have some sort of father figure as board chairman who is willing to counsel you about the outside world when it is absolutely necessary."

While there was no single father figure for Crozier, he was lucky enough to have several senior board members willing to provide him with guidance. "No one director ever told me what to do," he says. "They merely tried to understand the circumstances and tried to tell from their past experience how similar situations might apply. I was anxious to get the help. When I got stuck, I wanted help. I know some people, in some organizations, who don't want the help when they're in trouble. In fact, they seem to feel, somehow, that their manhood is at stake if they ask. It's a reflection of their ability to manage. I always assumed I had a resource out there—whether it was a staff member or a director—who could help adding to the sum total of the decision. I would have been nuts not to use them."

Crozier admits that he was fortunate that none of his requests for assistance ever produced a "Do this now or else" response. That kind of dictate, he explains, is "where the power gets taken away." Instead, he managed to balance his power of control with his associates' receptive attitude and influence powers to help the company make the necessary changes.

Crozier never forgot that although he had the power of control, the basic power always rested with the board. He was a young, feisty, talented CEO who had been brought in by a holding-company board. He says, "I would base my decisions on the collective wisdom I had gathered from my discussions with the different directors. The board had the power because I needed them behind me to do what I wanted to do. If you're brought in to change things, you're absolutely nuts not to use all the support you can get because, after all, these directors are the people who put you in this job, and if they're not going to support you, they can take you out."

While Crozier also likens the board/CEO relationship to a marriage—a partnership of power exchanges—he is quick to avoid sweeping generalizations. He says, "In reality, it is situational. It is absolutely company specific and situation specific. The most important thing a board does is pick a chief executive. When that happens, you have only so many executives available to you, even if you searched the realm at that particular point in time. And you only have certain kinds of directors with certain kinds of resources at that same point in time. It all comes down to a matter of personal chemistry, of respect."

The power partnership between the board and its CEO begins with that respect. And it is through respect that the balance remains intact. Over the years, Crozier has surprised some of his colleagues, and amazed some observers who did not know him well, by recruiting people to the BayBanks board that he knew would be difficult directors. He says, "People have said to me, 'You had a lot of guts to put so-and-so on your board.' To me, it's like playing a game. If you're not playing against good competition, you're not going to do much for yourself. I wanted people who were very strong in terms of sophisticated financial services. People who could keep me on my toes. It's different from the issue of a director with a manufacturing background who is dabbling in finance. We needed someone whose main street was finance and who would operate independently."

ORGANIZATIONAL POWER BALANCE IN CRISIS

I learned the importance of organizational power balance during a national emergency situation called World War II. The scene was Karnack, Texas, a land of scrub-pine, moss-covered forests. It was the domain of T. J. Taylor, landowner, justice of the peace, cotton farmer, grocer, general-store owner, distributor of his own currency, and father of Claudia Alta Taylor Johnson, better known later in her life as Lady Bird. Taylor ran Karnack as an economic, political, and social fiefdom unchecked until the government chose the town as its site for the Longhorn Ordnance Works.

The ordnance plant was dedicated to the manufacture of TNT (and, later, aircraft-launching rocket propellant) to meet wartime needs. Monsanto was doing its part for the country by taking on the contract of this government-owned facility and running the facility with its managers and technical staff. Along with a regiment of other Monsanto employees, I came to Texas for a four-year assignment.

This was a new kind of experience for me. At Monsanto, I had been managing larger and larger segments of operations. I'd gone from a lab into technical services. I had enjoyed a taste of marketing. Then I moved back into people management. It was the kind of entrepreneurial environment that encouraged people to step up to authority and to take on responsibility. Now I was working for the government. And the adventuresome spirit of Monsanto soon was sublimated not only by the safety precautions essential in the production of TNT but also by the rigid codes mandated by the Ordnance Department of the Department of Defense.

As plant manager, I dealt with a battery of administrative problems, with government relations, and a seemingly endless series of inspections. I coped with representatives from the Ordnance Department, general contractors, the Army Medical Corps, environmental safety inspectors and auditors, the Corps of Engineers, and the General Accounting Office. Just to make certain that the last drop of entrepreneurial energy had been sapped from my system, I also had to meet annually with negotiating teams from fourteen different labor unions at the same time. We had to teach T. J. Taylor's unskilled labor force what an honest day's work really meant. Retraining farmers to become skilled chemical plant workers dealing with alien matters of toxicity and explosiveness was a bit of hazardous duty that no one at Monsanto ever could have predicted.

The operating partnership was between the commanding officer, who represented both the ordnance department and the public's interest in the facility, and the plant manager, who represented the operating contractor's organization and its shareholders. In many ways, the relationship resembled the CEO/board pairing in real-world business. Our independent roles were equally important. The dependence on each other was mutual. And while accountabilities were separate and clearly defined, our obligations were mutual.

The primary power was the government's charge to make TNT, according to plan and according to cost. That was the imperative. They were the owner. We were the hired executive staff brought in to run the plant and to manage the operating staff. In Bill Crozier's analogy, they were the machine and we were the gasoline. They couldn't run their Ordnance Plant without us. And we certainly couldn't manage the logistics of getting the stuff to shell-loading plants and on to the troops—the end users, in peace-time consumer terms—without their tremendous network of transportation and facilities.

It was a reasonable model for any business. But this was not any business. It was a government business operating under the stress of wartime imperatives in a remote place: If you were designing a plant that could blow up, this was where you would put it. And this was a business that you might be sorely tempted to send sky-high if it weren't for the war. For starters, the Army likes to put everything in writing—everything. Everything that I approved, even if we already had a previous agreement on authority, expenditures, and resources, had to be run through a corps of accountants and legal people. When we had meetings, it would seem as if battalions had to show up for briefings before we could begin.

Because we were involved in a constant crunch, there were times when I would meet quietly with the commanding officer. We'd sit down to talk about a policy matter and it wouldn't be long before we had some sort of agreement. We were neighbors—the Monsanto personnel lived side-by-side with the top Army people in staff housing. This proximity helped us cut through a lot of red tape. It was that very convenience, however, that worked against us. Just as soon as we became comfortable with one new officer, the government would rotate him out. There was a kind of implicit government fear that the commanding officer would get to know the plant manager too well and the two would develop a collusion. So while we had some of the balanced elements of the power partnership in place, the officers' conclave of career captains and colonels kept moving in and out too quickly for us ever to become truly efficient.

For four years, no matter who the players were at any time, we all managed to put in about sixteen to eighteen hours a day to keep producing the TNT.

The people from Monsanto fulfilled their executive kinetic role: They took the power. The Army was in place as the latent power—the people who would manage the government bureaucracy and, in theory, free us up to take the action. The controlling interest was shared by the two parties, one acting as the CEO, the other as the board. The fulcrum was in place and the balance was established between the two parties.

It was a high-stress tightrope act to maintain the proper balance with turf, title, and tactics at stake. But it worked. No matter what the day-to-day problems might have been, we had a working model of the power partnership in place. An unqualified mandate from Washington to produce kept us busy. There was no CEO and director confusion as to what our purpose was. In that sense, the Karnack plant was a laboratory for corporate management. And the controlling interest—more specifically, the control power supported by influence power and appreciative power—worked to benefit the wartime effort.

THE POWER EQUATIONS

In thinking about power in pinstripes, it is helpful to look at the power retained and power delegated by the institution representing the enterprise. The power of the shareholders and the board of directors they elect can be characterized as *latent power*—power that is very real but not always evident. The managing director's (or chief executive's) power is *kinetic*—active demonstrative power that is evident in its regular use.

Ideally, the two types of corporate energy are complementary. When they overlap, it is only to reinforce each other.

In physics, this makes perfect sense. In business life, however, power does not merely exist. It can make its possessors possessed. In that unpredictable event—the corruption generated by power—the precision of physical science is useless. Only the concept of latent and kinetic power survives in the human laboratory.

There are three types of these powers which can be functionally represented by concentric circles. The first circle is *control power*—the power that an organization leadership has in controlling affairs and operations of the enterprise, such as budgets, the employees, the purpose of the enterprise, and the vision. The executive management in the form of the CEO (or managing director) is the person in responsible charge of this control aspect of power. Such control is specifically delegated by the board of directors to the CEO or managing director.

A concentric circle forming an annular ring around control power is what may be called *influence power*. This concerns the power that an executive group has to influence but not control elements surrounding it. This may involve the market, suppliers, public opinion, and sources of financing.

Extending the series of concentric circles of power further, the next annular ring (around control power and influence power) is called *appreciative power*. This term comes from the British military term, "enemy appreciation." This means that in a military campaign, a strategy, by definition, must determine (appreciate) prospective responses of the enemy to any action by the controlled group in order that their military strategy can be effective against opposing sources.

The board of directors is that part of the organization often most effective in looking at the external perspective. Such appreciative power is critical in rethinking and revitalizing a corporate strategy.

Appreciative power focuses any ambition-driven strategy to embrace condition-driven strategic considerations. The personal external networks of individual directors are invaluable in this regard. Proper use of advisory directors or advisory councils can also serve as a resource.

This perspective of three power equations was first hypothesized in May 1988 by William E. Smith, Ph.D., as a systems model for corporate governance. In his unpublished paper, "Extending Your Power: To Improve Your Organization's Performance," the author noted that, traditionally, organization is viewed as a structure from an internal actor's perspective. This is inadequate given contemporary business realities of external forces and competitive conditions. The limited use of power to control is not feasible in the current environment. It is impotent in obeying the unenforceable norms for effective governance given the external forces at work.

Smith concludes with the proposition that an enterprise which is using all three levels of power but is centered in a world of influence (as opposed to control) is constantly striving to (1) serve higher levels of purpose; (2) add more value to all stakeholders; and (3) learn from experience. If it succeeds, then it is more likely to cope with increased change, tougher competition, greater demands for social responsibility, and greater demands for ethical behavior.

Another concept of power is more militaristic and conventional. It is referred to as C^3I^2: command, control, communications, and intelligence (external) and internal orderliness.

This is often cited as a vital set of management processes. It is strange that little attention is given to the distinction between the respective zones of accountability, namely, the executive management level and the director's governance level of oversight.

The CEO may delegate functional responsibilities for the kinetic operation of the enterprise. This works well when the CEO delegates commensurate authority to carry out the respective executive and operational functions and tasks. But the CEO cannot delegate his accountability to the board of directors for the covenantal relationships required of an executive leader. These determine the enterprise culture, the tone-at-the-top, and the general corporate climate. The board of directors has the power and obligation to monitor these nonlegal, nonregulated attributes of an enterprise. Through the oversight of the executive management and the setting of an example of an informed, independent, and thoughtful group of willing fiduciaries, the latent power of the board provides oversight and monitoring of the enterprise.

Power Measurement

Numerous scholars have recognized and studied the importance of the power of the CEO and the board of directors. Very few strive to measure such power.

A relevant study was made of 1,763 senior managers in 102 of the largest firms in three industries (computer, chemical, and natural gas distribution) over a five-year period (1978–1982).[1] Power was defined as the capacity—with political skill and will—to influence strategic choices of an enterprise. The power dimensions applied in this research were structural power (hierarchical authority), ownership power (shareholders), expert power (managerial and advisory), and prestige power (elite education, personal status and reputation of key principals). Correlations in three studies for objective and perceptual measures of power added a fifth variable dimension, perceived power.

Interestingly, perceived power was correlated positively and significantly with structural, ownership, and prestige power. Not so with expert power. There was only a moderate correlation of expert power with perceived power.

The importance of top executive power in business organizations unsurprisingly identifies balance, distribution, and stability of power in the top team (including the CEO) as a major enterprise-specific variable. This confirms a commonsense, intuitive understanding of most experienced CEOs and directors. It further prompts the question, "What's new?"

Scholars have identified key power dimensions and provided one means of objective measurement and validation of the effectiveness of the executive team. Perhaps such methodology may help the CEO and the board in their empirical performance inquiries.

Power in Mortar Boards

Another research track on power and the college presidency extends our analytical framework of power in pinstripes to academic power in mortar boards. The Institute for Social Research at my alma mater in Ann Arbor, Michigan, recently studied the conventional major power types in educational enterprises, namely, leadership, authority, and influence. The forms of power, in ascending order of importance are as follows:

- *Coercive power,* which is the threat or use of punishment.
- *Reward power,* which involves the ability to reward.
- *Legitimate power,* which is the power of position.
- *Expert power,* which is based on the real or perceived knowledge of a leader.
- *Referent power,* or charisma, which is based either on a feeling of oneness with a leader or a desire for such a feeling. Charismatic leaders have an extraordinary ability to inspire trust, confidence, and performance.

The authors then set forth twenty-five recommendations for improving leadership in the college presidency. These are mindful measures that many for-profit enterprise leaders already make. There also is an edifying spin for the more profound and meditative province of higher education, with its concern over organizational power.[2]

The Hester Prynne Sanction

It is neither fallacious nor inappropriate to conclude this anchoring point with the concept of corporate shame.

Shame is one of the most noteworthy of artificial emotions. It is the result not of inbuilt and inherent feeling but of feeling implanted by the traditions and morals of the society in which the individual finds himself. The standards and types of thought in the various moralities of the world dictate the way in which shame is manifest in those parts of the world.

From Nathaniel Hawthorne's *The Scarlet Letter* (originally published in 1850):

The penalty thereof is death. But in their great mercy and tenderness of heart, they have doomed Mistress Prynne to stand only a space of three hours on the platform of the pillory, and then and thereafter, for the remainder of her natural life, to wear a mark of shame upon her bosom.

"A wise sentence!" remarked the stranger gravely bowing his head. "Thus she will be a living sermon against sin." (New York: Pocket Books, 1954)

Professor Peter A. French, in the essay, "Publicity and the Control of Corporate Conduct: Hester Prynne's New Image," argues that corporations as well as corporate individuals can and should be held morally responsible for untoward events of which they are intentional agents.[3] In our context, this means knowing disobedience to the unenforceable, covenantal relationships.

Further, French argues, guilty corporations can and "ought to be punished for their wrong doing"—the notion of adverse publicity as an alternate corporate punishment to be used to augment other sentences (fines, probation orders). The proposition is based on a social stigmatization thesis. French says, "Shame operates in the field of honor and self-respect rather than being associated with meeting legal and social obligations."

Professor French noted three business, press-reported examples of the impact of the power of shame. They are the following:

- The Allied Chemical Company's $13 million fine on 940 counts of polluting the James River, later reduced to $5 million when the company agreed to give $8 million to the Virginia Environmental Endowment.

- The Olin Mathieson Company's $45,000 fine after they agreed to set up a $500,000 New Haven Community Betterment Fund. The sentence was for a charge of conspiracy involving shipment of rifles to South Africa.

- A Nebraska corporation convicted of rigging bids in highway construction was ordered to donate $1.4 million to establish a permanent chair in business ethics at the state university.

One concluding consideration is that the great benefit of the Hester Prynne Sanction is its power to not only generate adverse publicity and social contempt, but to provide an incentive to adjust policy necessary for the corporation to regain "moral worth both in its own eyes and those of the community." Another consideration is that a possible fundamental problem is the uncritical assumption that the corporation is a moral person that will feel shame or be embarrassed.

The authors point out that it may well be that individual officers and directors of the corporation feel shame, but the corporation as an entity transcending the individuals within it will not, whatever feeling shame might mean with respect to a corporation.[4]

CEOs MAY NOT BE AS ENTRENCHED AS YOU THINK

The ability of chief executives to perpetuate themselves in power increases with their tenure and the number of inside directors on their boards. That's the conventional wisdom. But a study by William Ocasio, assistant professor at MIT's Sloan School of Management, challenges this thinking. Ocasio, who studied 225 CEO successions at 114 U.S. industrial corporations from 1960 to 1990, attacks many of the prevailing assumptions about entrenched CEOs and rubber-stamped boards.

"Corporations are places of shifting coalitions and incessant political struggles," Ocasio says. The longer CEOs are in power, the greater the chances are that their strategies and programs will fall out of sync with the company's operating environment, causing the company's performance to deteriorate and undermining their ability to hold together political coalitions.

Ocasio found statistical evidence that the turnover rate among chief executives increased rather than decreased with the length of a CEO's tenure. In other words, the longer CEOs stayed, the less secure was their hold on the job. Furthermore, someone who served on the board of a company before becoming its CEO was more likely to be replaced.

The turnover rate during rocky periods increased in relation to the board's size. "Larger boards increase the opportunities to forge coalitions to challenge the coalition led by the incumbent CEO," Ocasio says.

Ocasio found no statistically significant evidence that the greater the proportion of outside directors, the more likely it is that a board will replace the CEO during bad times. But there was significant evidence that a higher number of inside directors increases the rate of CEO turnover during such periods. "Insider board members serve several functions that may increase the rate of CEO succession under adversity," Ocasio says. "Insiders are obvious candidates for the CEOs position, and they have the in-depth information that the entire board may need to evaluate the CEO's explanations. In times of poor corporate performance, insiders may emerge as challengers to the CEO's authority and as rivals for the job."[5]

6

No Business like Closely Held Business: The Larger Parallel Economy

While trying to decide the most reasonable thing to do, privately owned firms sometimes behave very unreasonably. This particularly occurs with respect to obeying the unenforceable or norms of rational directorship. In part, this is because of the cognitive lenses through which closely held (or family owned) firm directors view their world.

Sense experience (gaining knowledge through our own five senses), intuition, and emotion tend to prevail over deductive logic, taking the word of others in authority (regulations, laws, societal norms), and synthetic scientific technologies of observation.

Closely held firms are no different in their decision making than broadly held, publicly owned firms, in most respects. The distinction, however, is in the reality that when closely held firms use poor judgment, they are still the final judge. The compensating feature is that their own assets, tangible and intangible, are at risk. When director-owners fail to consider the unenforceable, normative anchoring points in value judgment and decision making, they may be disadvantaged or damaged personally.

Family business or private business often is a long series of decisions the owners are not ready for. But time works great changes. Take the case of being an outside director of a family owned or closely held firm. As mentioned in the Preface, this category of business enterprise outnumbers publicly owned business in the United States by more than fifty to one, and is indeed a parallel economy. Real names were not used in the case histories that follow.

THE CEO OF THE MONTH[1]

Customhouse Mart, Inc., was started over forty years in upper Michigan by three college sophomore classmates as a full service, general retail store serving students and townspeople. The three founders, Stewart, Malcolm, and Anthony, formed the corporation owned by them and eventually their families. The covenantal relationships between the three founders were particularly strong.

Stewart, the eldest, provided financial smarts; Malcolm provided innovative marketing input; and Anthony handled personnel. Stewart was the nonexecutive chairman. Malcolm was the vice chairman and Anthony was the president. Machiavelli's observation prevailed: "It is not titles that reflect honour on men, but men on their titles." However, they could not agree on who would be CEO.

The team approach and plural management served the enterprise surprisingly well as it developed regionally. Approaching an $80 million revenue level in ten years, the company went public. The three founders and their families retained 40 percent ownership— sufficient to effectively control the firm and to elect two close business friends as outside directors. The three founders and their two friends constituted the board of directors, along with the corporate attorney. Two outside advisers were engaged as professional counsellors to the board to help with their personal networks on the east and west coasts.

The chain of stores diversified geographically under this talented management trio. However, plural leadership came on hard times. Each founder-principal pressed hard on his functional interest to the exclusion of the whole business strategy. Earnings drifted, competition began to take a toll. The outside directors and advisers were mildly critical, unhappy, but powerless to persuade the founder-director-managers to agree on one of them as CEO and to reorganize to fit managerial accountabilities of the total business.

Board meetings were interesting events. The vice chairman, Malcolm, was a born thespian and promoter. As the firm grew rapidly by acquiring regional theme retail stores, the board was informed of the acquisition proposal by a mock-up of the proposed target store. In one case, this was done by outfitting the boardroom as a boutique replica of the proposed retail acquisition.

I remember a board meeting in which a southwestern retail chain of three retail stores known for their leisurely, Western-style clothing was the acquisition that was up for approval. Cowboy hats of the proper size for each board member, along with a braided leather belt, were placed at each director's place around the board table. Promotional literature on the proposed acquisition was mounted on the walls of the boardroom as in a travel agency. Menus from the store's luncheon room appeared for the board lunch.

Malcolm could be enthusiastic and persuasive about any expansion plan as long as it included an acquisition of a new retail property. He was a born acquiror and a contagious one as far as the board was concerned. With all the razzle-dazzle presentations, Malcolm regularly got the board's support for the purchase of each business with little discussion of any downside of the acquisition. I was reminded of Oscar Wilde's comment that only an art auctioneer can be enthusiastic about all forms of art. Malcolm was a pushover for any new theme-related, retail enterprise. He captivated the board every time with his theatrical staging of the proposed acquisition's unique fashion or specialty attributes.

Despite declining earnings, the company's addictive acquisition plan occupied most of the board meeting time. Too little attention was paid to Customhouse Mart's overextended financial condition. The difference between an effective board and a benign board isn't that an effective board doesn't make poor decisions. An effective board just doesn't keep making poor decisions over and over again. Customhouse Mart's board kept authorizing more retail property acquisitions, many of which needed management talent which Customhouse Mart could not provide.

The two outside directors, supported by the two independent advisers, were unable to get the three principal owners to agree on who would assume overall responsible charge as the CEO accountable for all aspects of the business. A temporary solution was reached after three quarterly board sessions where tempers flared. A curious compromise was dreamed up by Stewart. He convinced Malcolm and Anthony of a rotating CEO position since none of them would defer to the others as the person to be in responsible charge. The advisers pointed out the hazards of this course but the three owner-manager-directors saw this scheme as the way to settle their own differences without resorting to agreement.

The three owners tried vainly to assume proper control of the business by taking turns being CEO for a month at a time. Within a period of six months, this shifting leadership caused subordinate management to play a game of waiting until the appropriate founder-director was in the CEO seat to make a proposal. Financial requests were delayed until the expansive, marketing-oriented founder became the CEO. Major personnel decisions were scheduled to catch the people-prone founder in responsible charge, and so on. The owners were unable to see this political picture while they were inside the frame. The captive outside directors were ineffective in generating any initiative or will to consider and correct the lack of introspection regarding such decision making and judgment processes, the unenforceable norms of good governance and good management necessary for an enterprise of this size and accountability.

Decision making at the executive management levels slowed down. Morale was adversely affected. Ambiguity prevailed as to who was in charge. The board meetings heated up as tension and conflicts arose over every board decision because of serious differences of opinion of the three founders. The outside directors remained impotent for too long.

Profitability drifted to such a point that the outside directors and advisers threatened to resign unless the three founders faced the reality that (1) their founding team model, modified with the rotating position of CEO, no longer adequately served the public corporation requirements for professional management; (2) management succession planning was nonexistent; and (3) the founders had to relinquish their confusing managerial roles and confine their input to the directorship level.

The good news came tardily but effectively. The founders agreed to give up executive roles and to serve only as directors. The title of founder-director was created to solve the ego problem. A newly elected, independent, nonexecutive chairman was elected. He was a retired, successful businessman who had just finished a three-year role as dean of a business school. When a CEO with demonstrated success in the retail business was recruited from another firm and elected to the board, a turnaround began to take place. The two advisory directors were replaced with a woman and a man elected as statutory directors. The woman was a professional from the retail industry. The man was an independent, experienced person from another service industry.

The only thing that saved Customhouse Mart from its plural management experiment was the ineffectiveness of this model beyond the early start-up of the enterprise. This first stage was an effective one of dependency on each founder's contributions. This prepared the firm for the development and a secure future, despite the scarcity of ready resources. The second stage of growth in earning power was exhilarating for the founders despite the imperatives of competitive business. Innovative business plans, a sense of identity, and team accomplishment held the principals and their company together through the exercise of going public. Their fortunes were then made. The third stage was somewhat free of the trammels and trauma of the second emergent stage. However, the founders were forced to implement anguished choices in order to achieve what some call the crown of life in their vocational period, rather than acquire extra years left over for retirement. Their covenantal relationships suffered.

These choices included agreement on relinquishing their individual goals of being CEO, agreeing on outside successor management, reorganizing the company so that the founders accepted "percussive sublimation"—being drummed upstairs to nonexecutive roles as members of the board. This stage of letting go of the executive management of the company satisfied the independent directors and the banks that were pressing the company to correct the drifting financial performances.

Perhaps the most significant decision by the founders was agreement to the change in size and composition of the board. The new board consisted of three founders and four outsiders, including the nonexecutive, nonfamily chairman, the new CEO, and the two other independent directors. The tone and conduct of the board meetings changed dramatically as this new board tackled the governance issues in an objective manner. The board wasn't a perfect one but it was effective.

Relieved of the pressures of ineffective, plural, executive management, the founder-directors soon began to enjoy their NIFO role (see Chapter 4). The separation of management from governance was complete as the controlling owners began to behave in their newfound directorship role. They performed as fiduciaries for all the shareowners and as overseers of the unenforceable, covenantal relationships between the directors and the executive management. Customhouse Mart stabilized and at last report was doing very well for its shareowners, customers, managers, and employees.

In some privately held business, the only way for the founders to express tribute is simply to leave the business alone. Stewart, Malcolm, and Anthony acknowledged that. Doing everything on the list of things a privately held company needs to do takes objectivity, trade-offs, and conviction. But most owners lack the objectivity and conviction to ever make the list. This is where independent directors and advisers contributed to solving the case of the CEO of the month.

LOVE IN THE BOARDROOM

The occasion was a two-day seminar in New Orleans on closely held company affairs. Twenty-one participants from fifteen firms were eager to learn and to share their family company triumphs and tribulations with others. While most attendees belonged to the membership association sponsoring the event, all present were strangers to each other except for the president and executive vice president of a family-owned trucking company, two fellow directors from a small, privately held insurance company, and the entire five-member board of the two-family owned DOD Component, Inc., located in a northwestern state.

It is often surprising how candid the discussions become in such a nonthreatening, workshop atmosphere of these membership association meetings. This occasion was no different. The exchange was lively, intimate, and even emotional at times. The focus of the exchange was on the covenantal relationships that were awry in their respective enterprises.

The introductory program covered basic principles of management and governance of small- to medium-sized companies. There were firms with controlling ownership privately held by families, founders, or, in one case, two-partner investors. Two of the companies had some minority public ownership. The focus of the seminar was on closely held company issues. This set the stage for a sort of group therapy session in which the participants were encouraged to describe their company and the opportunities and challenges facing them. Ideas on how to tackle vexatious problems before the fifteen different firms brought out perceptive and clairvoyant observations from the group.

The usual entanglement, conflicts, tensions, and reinforcements between family member interests and corporate interests were strongly evident. The willingness of everyone present to relate their company- or family-specific crises, concerns, and achievements was therapeutic in itself, due to the newfound intimacy and dynamics of the group.

The description by one vice president of a management succession problem was highly emotional. The second-generation competing members of the two family owners of this oil field services business made the rivalry of the Hatfields and McCoys seem tranquil. The young vice president was one of the two candidates for the presidency. He was facing a family board meeting later in the week and was grasping for any advice he might glean from others. The real problem was that the two different family aspirants were unwilling to work for the other. If there had been any kinship bonds in that boardroom, they had turned to hate of the virulent kind.

While the advice was varied, the underlying situation was insufficiently clear to achieve resolution by the discussion. However, the candidate's mind-set was improved by the independent perspectives and options offered by the group. I suspect his own career choice, regardless of the board's verdict, will be faced in a more reasoned manner than before the discussion.

The more intriguing fallout of the succession saga emerged during a coffee break. Helen was one of the two women directors of the DOD Components, Inc. She had some motherly advice to give the young officer of the oil field services company. At the coffee break, Helen came up to John, my colleague seminar leader, and chatted privately about the previous discussion of the rival family candidates for the presidency. "Isn't there any love in their boardroom?" queried Helen. This is definitely a covenantal matter in our professional businessman's vocabulary but is seldom expressed so poignantly.

John, taken aback by this question, fumbled over making an intelligent answer before escaping by calling the group back into session. This sensitive inquiry soon became better understood. Helen and her four fellow board members described their family company, DOD Components, Inc., and its succession issues with its first generation management and board of directors.

I asked Helen what DOD stood for. Her husband, Walter, intervened. "It's not Department of Defense, but we do service the military. It stands for Donaldson, Orson, and Donaldson, the three founders." Walter Donaldson, president at age thirty-seven, was the technical entrepreneur who created the business by developing specialized mechanical parts for automotive and aircraft controls. The market niche was apparently too small for larger component companies to be interested. DOD provided a servicing contract tailored to each customer which was responsive and reliable.

Dick Donaldson, an older brother, was the vice president of manufacturing. Although he had an engineering background, he became interested in the soft side of this $7 million revenue enterprise. His contributions to maintaining a family-style culture among the 480 employees, managers, directors, and owners were substantial. In some ways they were unique. Dick's wife, Helen, was employed in the administrative staff and helped support the caring and sharing climate which characterized the DOD style and texture of this firm.

Olle Orson, chairman of the board and CEO, was sixty-three years old and was an uncle to the Donaldsons, with prior experience in the automotive industry. Olle and his wife, Erika, were the fourth and fifth members of the board and owned one-third of the company stock. The two Donaldson brothers each held a third. Walter wanted to step out of the company and start up another high-tech enterprise around some novel, electronic consumer products he had conceived.

Olle had been with DOD since its founding in 1981. He had reached an age where he wished to relinquish his chairman and CEO role, remain on the board as a director, and pursue some outside interests of his and Erika's that had been waiting for their leisure and retirement time.

Dick was engrossed in his cultural values and belief system that had proven so effective in the nine years of rapid growth of DOD. One of his main worries was how to preserve the gestalt- and motivational-model company culture. DOD was expected to grow to $30 million revenue in the next ten years, according to their strategic plan.

In describing this collegial, communal, plural style of organizational responsibilities and method of conducting operations, the other DOD directors chimed in with their support of the importance of the founder-family-director-manager vision and mission of the company. Essentially it was to keep the size of the company below $10 million sales, and if the market was larger, to form one or more other small companies to be separately managed, hoping that the small-company cultural climate would remain intact. The issue of ownership of expanded operations in this multiple, small-company complex had not been addressed sufficiently to answer questions about maintaining motivational drives in the proposed small-unit model concept.

Dick Donaldson shared the company organization charts and structural concepts with the seminar group. His representation featured the well-researched social science model of an inverted pyramid, placing the employees and customers at the apex and the owners, directors, and managers as foundation blocks. The founders' vision, objectives, ethics, creed, ideology, and philosophy revealed strong humanistic overtones (and some cosmological ones). The model provided the base for creating and empowering the organization to follow family values, canons, and precepts in conduct of the corporation.

The company was small enough to retain person-to-person contacts between the founders, directors, and top management team, all of whom were members or descendants of the original entrepreneurs and investors. Employees were well paid, and benefits were better than those of competing companies and community norms. The workforce was nonunion.

The organizational symbols, information paths, functional relationships, and power flows, from the share owners up the organization to the customers and employees, were new age in style. They could be described as a nonlinear, direct, network type of process achievable in small family, or peer group membership and cooperative groups. Charismatic leadership and a caring and sharing tone to all company activities and communications were apparently working very effectively for DOD at this stage of its corporate existence.

The key issue was revealed by the disclosure that two of the principal owners wanted to let go of their executive and functional roles. They indicated a desire to repot themselves and their emotional investment in other endeavors of greater interest at this stage of their lives. In small family firms, this rite of passage often comes with a generational change, either as the second generation, or more frequently, as the third generation becomes eligible to take over the family business or wishes to opt out of the family-controlled environment.

No conflict, tension, or adversarial dimension of the two-family leadership was evident. The problem was how to preserve DOD's small size and effective family culture if two of the five directors removed themselves from active roles in the corporation.

The company condition reminded me of early forms of social organization that evolved in antiquity as the nuclear family became an extended family unit—a tribe or clan where egalitarianism prevailed and territory, bounty of the hunt, yield from the harvest, or any possessions were the property of the group, shared equally.

As civilization advanced and became more complex, the right to private property evolved. Communal groups became more formally structured and organized. Original cultural values were preserved in some larger social groupings. Personal relationships often suffered due to bureaucratic barriers and a diminished sense of belonging. Self-esteem and self-actualization got caught up in political and impersonal forces common to complex, more technological, economically oriented, and competitive environments. Orwellian cultures in society, industry, and governmental sectors replaced many of the extended family values, and motivation often was suppressed by the company cultures. A proper balance of professional, functional management and human, Renaissance-style environments became more difficult to achieve in large organizations.

Dick Donaldson and his associates in DOD had something special in their new-age type of company organization. But the expressed desire of two of the principal molders of this culture presented a significant challenge.

Normally, closely held company crises move through three stages: (1) the crisis of finding the founder-owners' successors, (2) the crisis of reorganization under new leadership, and (3) the crisis of the original owners and principals letting go of their dominant hold on the enterprise.

In DOD's case, the third crisis was appearing first. Two of the key leaders wanted to let go before successors and reorganization had taken place. Success of the company in terms of rapid growth complicated the situation. Expected increase in company size threatened the family style of governing and managing the company. There was the need to first restructure the organization and its control and command processes. Hierarchy, rather than a horizontal organizational network, was beginning to appear and threaten the egalitarian culture. Differences of opinion among the principals was somewhat evident during the interrogation session with the other participants at the seminar.

I detected some understanding of the need for, and value of, one or more outside, independent directors added to their family board to help guide them in the immediate years ahead. Whether the implant of independent directors on the board would cool off some of the bonding of family and employees remains to be seen.

Helen was correct in one sense; many companies could use love in their boardroom provided it is practical love, including the values and determining attitudes for enterprise leadership. It is manifest in covenantal relationships rather than contractual relationships. Practical love provides what the 1989 Treadway Commission on corporate conduct calls the need for a proper tone at the top to keep institutions serving their owners and having consideration for the stakeholders in the society in which the corporations compete economically.

THE SAGA OF FIRMAN BERGDÄHL

Bergdähl and Company, a family specialty furniture business, was incorporated in 1890 in the town of Vaggeryd, near the middle of southern Sweden in an area known as Götaland. This is a small community and the location is better known as the area from which more than a thousand people emigrated to the United States during the late 1860s. The famine in Sweden was due to failure of potato and other crops. Vaggeryd is an agricultural site. Bergdähl and Company is one of the few manufacturing enterprises.

Ernst-Viktor Bergdähl founded firman Bergdähl (the company known as Bergdähl or Hill Valley). From a business standpoint, it was the worst of times. Many small family firms in the region were heading for bankruptcy due to the depressed economic conditions and underdeveloped potential of that Swedish territory. Ernst-Viktor, with Walloon blood ingrained with his Viking character, was of stern Lutheran Protestant stock.

The saga occurred at a time when religious values were dominant as a sacred-value framework for the profane domain of commerce. Ernst-Viktor was fond of quoting Carlyle: "No man has worked, or can work, except religiously." You worked and attended church until you died; otherwise you didn't eat.

Ernst-Viktor refused to compromise with his conscientious belief that business and social welfare are partners. In defending his commitment to social responsibility of both family and firm, he would often repeat Martin Luther's famous words: "Here I stand; I can do no other." The family, the church, the community, and his business were one.

Over time, most villagers became dependent, directly or indirectly, upon the prosperity of Ernst-Viktor's family-owned enterprise. The company grew slowly but steadily, driven by the charismatic, single-handed leadership and craftsmanship of the founder. The firm developed and Ernst-Viktor controlled all company activities personally with a team-relationship style. However, there was no doubt who was in charge. Ernst-Viktor, through his expertise, his management by walking around (MBWA) approach, and his charismatic handling of people, became the rallying point for all employee-relations matters and all business, strategic, and policy decisions.

Authoritarian fiats were explicitly absent in dealing with nonfamily employees; they were strongly present in his family relations on and off the job. Members of the family were employed in the business, as were other villagers.

The company's specialty—handmade home furniture and, later, office furniture—became the Tiffany-grade products of Sweden. The firm remained small, focusing on high quality and originally designed products. These were produced in lots of a hundred or less, rather than the thousand-lot batches manufactured by the large, automated furniture competitors. Before the 1950s when air travel overtook travel by sea, Bergdähl handmade furniture was a feature of the Swedish–American luxury passenger vessels.

The familial-patriarch family culture has been successfully maintained in the business through four generations of family ownership and leadership. In recent years, revenues stabilized at $1.5 million to $2.0 million (Swedish Kroner equivalent). By plan, the family limits growth of the business in order to retain family values, social climate, and specialty market position. Head count has never been over 100 full-time employees. All facilities are at the single, original factory location in a picture-book, bucolic setting near a small lake, not far from the city hall which also serves as headquarters of the Swedish commune.

Through the years, as competition and customer preferences changed, Bergdähl and company was innovative and adaptive in keeping costs under control and avoiding an administrative bureaucracy. Sound strategic and defensive measures were employed to retain the master-craftsman image and handmade distinction of high-quality furniture lines. Cost savings were achieved by one marginal production compromise. Reluctantly, furniture table and chair legs were made using woodworking machinery. All other furniture components remain handcrafted. Wood-carving skills are handed down from Ernst-Viktor's early role as master craftsman and designer.

Another strategic change helped keep the company competitive. In order to keep overhead costs down and tap outside talent, he discontinued furniture design within the company. All designs are now purchased from outside design groups.

The woodcarver apprentice system involved the son working for the father as an early teen until Ernst-Viktor considered him accomplished and old enough to work alone. He then took on an extended-family apprentice of his own, or nonfamily associates as the firm got larger. This rite of passage was a tribal-like event. It usually took place in the apprentice's late twenties. It was marked by a factory ceremony and an increase in wages. Elite professional ranking of master craftsman was an initiation amongst fellow workers, office staff, and the few managing lead craftsmen. Achieving Ernst-Viktor's approbation and peer acceptance was the significant motivational force in this extended family culture. The heritage remained so into the fifth-generation family cycle of ownership. It was at that point that I became acquainted with Olle, a member of the Bergdähl clan. Interestingly, he had not pursued the family business but was very proud of his family's achievements.

Olle is now in his middle forties. He is a successful chief executive of a Swedish, publicly owned, medium-sized specialty chemical company. I had the privilege of being on the advisory board of his company. We had frequent business relationships, and I had occasional personal contact with his family. Through these associations, I came to know and be fascinated by the genealogical success saga of firman Bergdähl; how family values, vision, and kinship bonds successfully coped with three crises of family-firm ownership.

These three crises are well-established rites of passage for family businesses and their owners. The first is coping with management succession. The second crisis is reorganizing the business, post-leadership succession. The third and most anguished—often ineluctable—crisis that family leaders face is that of letting go when generational changes take place or external factors alter effective control of the business.

Normally, in each of these three crises, the value of independent, nonfamily, professional advice and trusted counsel from sources with no beneficial interest is often a fulcrum. It can aid in forcing an emotion-laden choice of transfer of power, in facilitating an objective restructuring of the business, including redefinition of roles (if any) of family members in the enterprise, and in bringing about a dignified, sensitive, unambiguous decoupling of those family members in powerful positions from their roles of being in responsible charge, or having accountability for, performance of the business. This includes being a director of the company, an emeritus director, an executive or ex-chairman, a corporate consultant, or an adviser.

However, firman Bergdähl handled the transformations with a minimum of outside advice. They surmounted the crises relying essentially on family wisdom plus some professional help from a local banker and local attorney. Both of these nonfamily members of the board had inherent conflicts of interest in their banking and legal services for the firm, but their influence on policy was minimal. The company survived and prospered by the strong will and hands of the founder. He was both wise and smart enough to integrate the family's and the enterprise's interests. This strong family-business texture and philosophy has carried the firm into its fifth generation of owner-managers. But there are more interesting family sidelights of the Bergdähl saga.

The villagers considered Ernst-Viktor a man of heart. His firm provided employment and social and economic benefits for many in the local community. He was lord, mayor, and czar in economic affairs of the commune. The Bergdähl clan, through intermarriage, was active in most of the religious, social, and political activities of greater Vaggeryd.

Ernst-Viktor, our Swedish, family-business leader role model, was an imposing personality. He was tall and stately. He wore contemporary round spectacles, had distinguished grey hair, sported a barbershop moustache, and exhibited a stern, strict manner. You spoke to him only when spoken to. These personal characteristics were passed along from generation to generation. My friend Olle recounted that he was seven years old before his father, Göran, Ernst-Viktor's middle son, even spoke to Olle. Women were to stay at home and raise the children until the children were ready to brave the world.

A family story that Olle shared with me illustrated Ernst-Viktor's dedication to tradition and his expectation that as head of the family, he would be served well by all members. This expectation spilled over to everyone who worked in the company, related or nonfamily.

Ernst-Viktor was a creature of his own habits. He left the factory daily at eleven o'clock and walked the mile to his home to have his morning coffee and *kuchen*, served by his wife or daughter, in the kitchen with table setting. One day he went home as usual and entered the kitchen to find no one there. The table was set, the coffee cup and cake were in place, and hot coffee was on the stove, but no one was there to serve him. He sat down and waited in vain for someone to appear. Finally, he got up and strode back to the factory without serving himself!

Ernst-Viktor had been brought up in an era where, as leader of the family, he looked out for everyone. In turn, he expected to be served. The only avocation he had was bee-keeping. He was strict with wife and children and expected siblings to do what they were told and only then. When he died in 1948, his wife never remarried. She carried on as the primary family figure.

Ernst-Viktor's instructions for succession put Sven, the youngest of three sons, in charge of the business. The basis was his father's opinion that he was the most apt to wear the mantle. Göran became a schoolteacher at Ernst-Viktor's direction. The eldest son, Haralt, was not in the business or on the board. Haralt had a mental problem—ablutomania. He was obsessed with cleanliness of himself, requiring incessant and compulsive washing. Working at any task was hampered by cleanup rituals repeated endlessly. Haralt marked and survived awhile but eventually became insane and was committed to the local asylum.

Of the founder's two daughters, only the older one, Dagmar, worked in the business. Today the company is led by Haralt's grandson, Jesper II, a third-generation sibling not as intellectual as his grandfather but self-educated and industrious. Dagmar, unmarried, is retired and still on the board at age eighty-five, after serving in the factory office for forty years.

Incidentally, the office is a most modest one. The founder's creed was to stay out of the offices and spend work time in the factory carving ornamental furniture—the lifeblood of the firm. Hard physical work, close attention to money matters, and minimum office force were essentials for a profitable furniture business.

The board of directors consists of Jesper, Dagmar, Göran's cousin by marriage, Ralph, who worked in a bank, and Lars, the family attorney. Board meetings are routine. Critical business matters are decided in family gatherings and ratified in the infrequent, short, formal directors' meetings.

The company continues to be profitable. The work climate and traditions are more or less maintained. Firman Bergdähl survived the unusually critical transition, passing through the third-generation succession and adjustment. This is a tribute to the founder's vision, work ethic, creed, and commitment to high quality, handcrafted production, selection of quality materials and designs, and the pursuit of a niche business strategy. It has constantly driven the firm from its modest beginning.

Ernst-Viktor followed Confucius's advice: "It is not possible for one to teach others, who cannot teach his own family." He taught this family what the French religious historian Ernst Renan (1823–1892) believed: "The family virtues are indispensable to the proper continuance of a society." Family virtues were synonymous with family business virtues in the following ways:

- The head of the family business must create and maintain the family culture and then struggle with self-identity and changing role expectations.

- Culture of the family firm plays an important role in determining success of the business beyond the first generation.

- Succession planning is necessary for first-generation family firms to survive their founders. Subsequent successions may become even greater challenges.

- Superior quality product (or service) paces competitive positioning of a firm.

- Although formal planning is absent in many family firms, objective, strategic thinking by the family and, particularly, the family-company head is necessary for success.

- A family system rather than management system can be a key integrator of a family firm. The system may not necessarily detach the board of director's role from family-council roles. But the board-level decisions must be objective and realistically separate business matters from family interests.

THE LOVABLE THIEF

Robert Benchley once opined, "The son-in-law also rises." This, of course, refers to the form of nepotism in which a family brings a member of the extended family, such as an in-law, into the family business. This practice can create what is often considered by nonfamily employees as a discriminatory policy and a constraint on their career paths. In the following saga of nepotism, some unusual events took place.

The F. T. Corporation with headquarters in Iowa was a very successful family business. It started in 1939 as a manufacturer of farm tools and small-sized equipment. Jim Hazeltine was the well-educated son of a well-to-do farming family. After graduating from college and after the Depression, he elected not to continue in the farming business but to start his own manufacturing firm, dedicated to making and selling the finest farm tools and associated products. The product line included wheelbarrows, workshop hand tools, ladders, scaffolding, and similar small- to medium-sized equipment not requiring large capital investment in factory facilities.

The company was originally called the Farm Tool Firm, but the name was changed to the F. T. Corporation as the firm grew in size and became diversified. By 1989, F. T. Corporation had grown to over $200 million revenue and had expanded into several midwestern states for manufacturing sites. The company had acquired and expanded a chain of retail hardware stores throughout the midwest and was very profitable.

The ownership of F. T. Corporation was closely held by Jim as CEO, and his wife, Laura, had financial control. After earning an MBA degree at Duquesne University, their son, Mark, worked up to vice president of marketing in the family firm and was a minority shareholder. Their daughter, Hanna, was not engaged in the business and had married Larry Grant, a childhood sweetheart. Larry was a favorite of the Hazeltine family, a star athlete in high school and big man on campus at Iowa State, where he graduated with an MBA. Jim invited Larry into the family firm and quickly made him vice president of administration, including accounting, public relations, and the personnel function. Larry's poise and social skills made him a favorite of everyone in the executive management, the office staff, and every member of the Hazeltine family. Larry was given a small amount of stock.

The other minority shareholders were two old friends of the family who had invested some money in the venture when Jim started the firm in 1939. Members of the board were Jim, Laura, Hanna, and Mark. All shareowners were satisfied with the return on their investment, the dividend payout, and the growth in shareholder value.

The outlook for the company never looked better when Jim and Mark Hazeltine came to talk to me and Ben, a close friend of mine and a lawyer from our University of Michigan days. Ben and I had been members of the same social fraternity, Sigma Phi Epsilon. We had lived together for two years at the fraternity house on Washtenaw Avenue in Ann Arbor and had kept in touch all during our business careers, his in Iowa and mine in Massachusetts.

Through another Sig Ep network connection, Ben had known of the F. T. Corporation and its successful growth. His law firm also had done some corporate legal work for them over the years. Ben had built his own law practice around family enterprises. It was logical for him to be approached by Jim Hazeltine in connection with a delicate family firm crisis. Ben asked me to help him in advising Jim and Mark Hazeltine.

The first revelation came at a dinner meeting with Jim and Mark at the Blackstone Hotel in Chicago, where Ben and I learned about the extraordinary situation, one I had never heard about before, and I hope I hear of no other such family firm crisis again.

Jim, now age 72, came right to the point. The CPA auditors had uncovered substantial embezzlement of cash from the company. The thief was revealed to be son-in-law Larry Grant. Admired by all, Larry was loved dearly by Jim's daughter, Hanna, and Jim's two granddaughters. Laura had the greatest pride in her son-in-law. But Mark's position was adamant. Larry had been caught stealing and had admitted it in an anguished session with him and Jim. Larry should be fired and prosecuted as any other criminal. His in-law status was a family affair and did not transcend the business role and issue of embezzlement and accountability.

Jim, drawn and weary, was not so sure this was the solution. At this point in time, only the auditors, Mark, Jim, and Larry knew of the discovery. The amount of money involved was substantial as the embezzlement had been taking place over the last six years. The crime had been discovered by the auditors when they found some incriminating evidence of accounting record changes and claims from customers who had paid F. T. Corporation but had not received the purchased goods.

Jim was deeply concerned about the impact that public revelation of the findings would have on the families, the firm, customer and supplier relations, the banks, and, most of all, his only daughter, Hanna, and his grandchildren.

Jim then confided that the auditors had discovered the embezzlement several months before and that he had had a confrontation with Larry, who broke down and admitted to his transgressions.

Larry also agreed to some psychiatric counseling and vowed he would provide restitution and completely reform his errant ways. After discussions with the counselor, Jim believed that this illness was likely to reoccur, similar to the pattern followed by many addicted alcoholics and gamblers who possessed a serious character fault.

Jim was not willing to fire Larry and allow him to work for someone else, knowing his character weakness (putting his hand in the till). Larry was well compensated and had everything going for him career-wise, family-wise, and estate planning-wise. He had the most important asset of a loving and considerate wife, loving mother- and father-in-law, and a key position in a trusting family-style company. This culture had been maintained throughout the growth of F. T. Corporation.

To complicate matters, there were serious tax problems to resolve. Amended tax returns for the past six years would have to be filed. Supplier and customer accounts would have to be reconciled and adjusted. Inventory accounts needed attention.

The family dilemma was vexatious. Jim's preference was to keep Larry in the company and give him time to mend his ways and to pay back the embezzled funds. The latter step would take several years. Mark's preference was to fire Larry, prosecute him as with any other criminal, and let the family weather the crisis.

We offered several suggestions, none of which were enthusiastically embraced by both Jim and Mark. One suggestion did seem to be the best course to them. To assuage Jim's concern for helping his only son-in-law and, more poignantly, his daughter's and his grandchildren's reputation and family situation, we suggested the affair be kept confidential and that Larry be moved out of the mainstream of F. T. Corporation activities. He would be assigned to doing some public and customer relations work with no access to corporate funds to tempt him. He would be relocated to another of the company offices away from headquarters. Larry would, in return, pledge restitution of the money with interest and agree to continue with appropriate counselors to help him overcome his problem. Larry had diverted company funds into some personal real estate and securities investments in a private bank and brokerage account in Chicago, where he frequently visited on business and attended professional accounting and management meetings.

After considerable and careful discussion with the CPA firm and tax authorities, and taking care of the overdue customer and supplier commitments, an arrangement was worked out with Larry. Mark was not satisfied with the soft treatment but was prevailed

upon to agree with this course of action by the pleading of his father and, particularly, by the anguished requests from his mother
and sister, who finally had to be informed.

This career repotting was achieved with minimum disruption over
a six-week period and was masked somewhat by coincidental reorganization and management development, and rotating assignments
worked out for the executive group and the retail franchisee group
executive.

In checking on how the changes worked out and how Larry and his
family were faring a year after this change, it was good news to
hear that Larry had apparently gone straight. The bad news was that
Larry had been unable to bear the confidential stigma of his transgressions as a member of the family and an executive of the firm.

Hanna was a loyal and faithful wife and helped to the end. The
professional counseling was also very effective in helping Larry re-
cover. However, he elected to leave the company and relocate his
family in connection with another job in retail store management in
a West Chicago suburb. At last report, his repayment of funds was
on schedule. He and his family were reasonably well adjusted outside the family circle.

Larry possessed a winning personality and an enlarged ego. He had
been so likeable and popular with the family, in school, and in business that he assumed there was always a free lunch and free lunch
money for a charmer and an opportunist. Whether Jim was correct in
his character assessment may not be known for some time. Jim believed Larry was an addicted, slick, but lovable crook. He felt obligated not to lose control of Larry's career for concern over what he
might do to another company in another situation. Jim was disap-
pointed that Larry, Hanna, and the family were now out of his parental influence, but he could only hope for full recovery on Larry's part.

The lovable thief may well be completely reformed and well on
the way to becoming a son-in-law to be proud of, but he is working
in another business. The final episode is yet to be written.

CLOSELY HELD BUSINESS DIRECTORSHIP

In the design, description, and behavior theory of organization,
scholars have identified at least a hundred input variables that are
unrelated to each other and yet are important. About fifty structure
variables, thirty function variables, and close to twenty output vari-

ables are also involved and are relatable to each other. The specification and classification of these two hundred or so variables which make a difference is complicated, indeed.

Closely held business, including family controlled business, is a diverse, variable-rich species of organization. Variety ranges from the minimum formation of a mom-and-pop family firm, sole proprietorships, and partnerships to the sophisticated corporate complex of publicly traded, Fortune 100, family-controlled industrial, retail, or business giants, such as Cargill, Ford, du Pont, Levi Strauss, Campbell Soup, Johnson & Johnson, Syms (a New Jersey discount clothing chain), Louisville's *Courier-Journal,* the Newhouse family company, Advance Publications, *FORBES* Magazine, and Carlson Companies service conglomerate.

Such enduring and successfully controlled enterprises develop an enterprise-specific system to take care of their own species. This treasures the owner's heritage and vision for the firm, a tribal group-value system, ethical and moral codes of conduct, company philosophy, operating creed, social norms, and a professional process of governing and managing the enterprise. Such stewardship guides the enterprise in a competitive environment with proper regard for fiducial and stakeholder obligations to all its constituents: shareowners, family-related and nonfamily investors, and all those parties or partners who are concerned with or affected by the conduct of the business.

PERENNIAL MANAGEMENT AND GOVERNANCE ISSUES

A plethora of issues is experienced by family firms, partnerships, and closely held enterprises. Many of these may become complex, painful, vexatious, and anguished issues. The logical, rational, impersonal, and linear-type issues of the business system are tangled up with personalities, nonlinear type issues of feelings, egos, emotions, individual interests, and expectations. There are many patterns to characterize kinship-bonded, partnership, ethnic, religious, modern-tribal value systems and cultures in a generalized way. The patterns express dilemmas which require reconciliation by combining values and making many choices that are not either-or choices but are both-and choices. Some outside, independent, professional directorship may be required to achieve this.

Some issues are less emotionally tainted by the closely held enterprise culture and are more concerned with the professional business system. These may include publicity shyness and secrecy about the business; business control problems; the flight to exaggerated uniqueness at the expense of profitability; the inner-direction factor of neglecting external trends and the market; problems of succession, reorganization, and letting go of the business; tax and estate problems; questions of over and underpayment of controlling members; value of outside-the-firm apprenticeship for key executive members before they assume responsible positions; career positioning of the three types of founders (proprietors, conductors, and technicians); conflicts over ownership changes; business mission versus the controlling owner's mission; professional management and governance standards, including criteria for business development; and the controlling owner's effect on investment decisions (e.g., concentration of shares in a limited number of management's hands).

Professional management and governance can address these issues. They can also do the following:

- Lead to a stronger sense of mission
- Lead to well-defined, longer term goals
- Lead to either enhanced or diminished self-analysis
- Bring out the best in employees
- Provide foresight for the business
- Require more (or less) bureaucracy
- Minimize office politics as distinct from family politics

Perhaps this chapter can be concluded best with the following professional observation from Abraham Myerson (1881–1988), M.D., a Russian-born, former clinical professor of psychiatry at Harvard Medical School: "Man uses his intelligence less in the care of his own species than he does in his care of anything else he owns or governs."

7

Trousers of Decorum: Cover-Your-Backside Ethics

Every man has his moral backside as well, which he does not expose unnecessarily, but keeps covered as long as possible with the trousers of decorum.
—Georg Christoph Lichtenberg (1742–1799)
German physicist and satirist

Anguished ethics is the apt labeling given applied ethics by the pre-eminent pioneer in the field of business ethics. I had the privilege of knowing Dr. Clarence C. Walton when he was president of Catholic University of America in Washington, D.C. Clarence's influence during academic and administrative duties at Columbia University, at the American College (Bryn Mawr), and in executive programs with major corporations and associations enriched my own and many others' directorship practice and executive management. He was profound about all sides of the moral manager. I've applied Clarence's teachings to my own experience with business ethics dilemmas.[1]

There are a half-dozen tales from my own ethics casebook in this chapter. Some are oldies. Others required Solomonesque solutions to be made in recent boardrooms in which I served or with which I became familiar. After these cases, I include some touchstones on how to cope with the ethical and moral issues involved. The solutions vary widely depending on personal, organizational, external, environmental, legal, and cultural variations in ethics, value systems, beliefs, attitudes, and articles of faith, whether your trousers of decorum remain up or down.

The cases have been clinically debated in very lively workshops conducted at (1) governance reform seminars in Hungary, racially dominated by descendants of the Magyar of Finno-Ugric stock, plus some elements of Turkish and Bulgarian values; (2) the Malaysian Institute of Management positioned in Kuala Lumpur surrounded by four separate ethnic groups, namely, the Aborigines, Malays, Indians, and Chinese; (3) the Singapore Institute of Management, in a rapidly developing country that has been called Instant Asia because so many cultures intermingle there; (4) Trinidad, one of the most prosperous Caribbean countries having many nationalities and creeds with equal numbers of African and East Indian descent as the two main groups; and (5) regular and continuing series of seminars sponsored by professional associations and educational groups in the United States.

Some thoughts on protocols for prescriptive ethical decisions follow the cases.

The Case of the Art of British Diplomacy   This question is posed by Allan Bloom, professor in the Committee of Social Thought, University of Chicago: If you had been a British administrator in India, would you have let the natives under your governance burn the widow at the funeral of a man who died?

The Case of the Leaning Tower Tactics, Italian Style   You are the chief financial officer (CFO) of an international company with a majority-owned Italian subsidiary. The subsidiary is about to sign a large profitable contract for providing goods and services to a state-owned enterprise. The size of the contract commitment is such that it requires board approval.

A facilitation payment in the form of a kickback to an individual is part of the deal. Local legal counsel advise that the extra payment is not unusual and in accord with Italian practice. From a U.S. point of view, the size of the payment is not out of line with past facilitating payments in Italy.

Would you advise your managing director (MD) of this requirement of the deal? If the MD wishes not to reveal this feature to the board, would you, as the CFO, advise the chairman of the audit committee or other members of the Board? If, as the CFO, you were a director of the parent company or of the Italian subsidiary, would this make any difference in your decision and action?

The Greek Proverb Case   *First secure an independent income, then practice virtue.* You are the CFO of a medium-sized, closely held, publicly traded (over-the-counter) company. Your chairman and CEO wants a deferred, unrestricted compensation package that is also a current deductible corporation expense and nontaxable to him until he receives it. The chairman does not want this to come to the attention of the board. He is the controlling shareowner.

Would you accede to the chairman's request? Would you advise the audit committee or other members of the board of any concern you have over the request?

The Case of Call to Arms   You serve as the vice president of research and development (R&D) of a major publicly traded sporting goods company. The company has a small arms subsidiary. The subsidiary has developed a new, plastic, high-rate-of-fire handgun with a large estimated market potential. However, it has been repeatedly rumored that your CEO will not let this product be brought to market because of his deep conviction about preventing general sales of handguns to the public as a deterrent to crime in the nation.

Would you let this secret decision of your CEO go unchallenged? Would you inform the chairman or other members of the board? Would it make any difference if you were also a director as well as the vice president of R&D of this company?

The Case of the Way Things Are Done in the European Economic Community (EEC)   You are the vice president of human relations of a privately held U.S. multinational company in the services industry. The CEO advises you that he has agreed to pay $400,000 as severance pay to a senior vice president. The CEO is terminating her services because of unethical price-fixing practices. The payment is to be made offshore so that it will not be readily apparent or reported to the tax authorities.

Do you challenge the CEO on this arrangement? If the CEO instructs you, as the vice president of Human Resources, to proceed anyway, would you bring this to the attention of the audit committee? Would your answer be different if the individual is the president of the parent company's subsidiary located in the EEC?

The Case of Morality Is Drawing the Line Somewhere   British journalist Gilbert Keith Chesterton (1874–1936) asserted that private ethical values inevitably affect corporate decisions.

As the chief accounting officer (CAO) of a publicly traded company, you have become aware of a material fault in one of the company's products. In the near term, this will cause a recall and abandonment of a sizable inventory.

The most appropriate accounting treatment would be to provide a reserve for such an event. The CEO tells you not to provide such a reserve. The auditors have not found out about this situation on their own.

Do you, as the CAO, go to the chairman of the audit committee and tell him or her? Would it make any difference if you, the CAO, were on the board?

The Case of the Family Ferry Tale   This apocryphal and nonbusiness fable was first heard at Lake Moraine, Hamilton, New York, at AMA's Operation Enterprise. The program is an innovative practicum designed about thirty years ago for enhancing high school senior's and college freshman's understanding of our democratic, free-enterprise system. Experienced managers do the instructing and surrogate parenting during two weeks of camp recreation and learning.

I have used this fable at many board director and executive management seminars, plus intimate family gatherings. It has never failed to get a spirited, diverse response. For example, in Trinidad, a business leader and his working son participated jointly. After the case study, the father, somewhat rattled, confided in me that it was apparent that he really didn't understand his son nor the younger generation's sense of ethical and moral values—their moral decorum. This is the ferry tale.

Emerald Isle and Pine Isle were two small islands in a remote sea off the Latin American coast. The water between was infested with piranha fish that often attack men and large animals.

A lovely, young maiden, Mary, lived on Pine Isle with her mother. Mary's true love, Joseph, moved to live on Emerald Isle. Disconsolate over never getting to see Joseph again, Mary stood dejectedly at the water's edge considering whether to plunge in and give up.

Now appears Steve, a young swain acquaintance to whom Mary told her morbid thoughts over her plight.

Entrepreneur Steve suggested he could ferry Mary to Emerald Isle in his rowboat on one condition: She would sleep with him that night.

Disconcerted, Mary retreated to seek her mother, and she told her all. Her mother responded, "Mary, ever since your father died, I strived to have you make decisions on your own. You know how your family has lived our lives. You make up your own mind." Nonplussed, Mary lay awake most of the night. In the morning she told Steve she would accept the deal.

When Mary reached Emerald Isle, she rushed into Joseph's arms and told him all, including her means of getting there. Joseph's reaction was harsh, harrowing, but resolute. He said, "Mary, I never want to see you again." Rejected, dismayed, and despondent, Mary again walked to the shore contemplating ending it all.

And now appears Marcus, who discovers Mary just in time. After hearing Mary's story, Marcus says, "Mary, I'll marry you." The ferry tale ends here as far as this moral and ethical case study is concerned.

The following is a question test for all engaged in hearing this fable, whether intimate family, friends, directors, business, or professional persons: Privately rank the five actors (Mary, Mother, Steve, Joseph, and Marcus) in decreasing order of ethical and moral behavior, the most ethical and moral person being number one, the least being number five; compare the rankings and defend your choice.

THE ETHICAL ALGORITHM SOLUTION

The preceding anguished ethics cases from my own ethics casebook focus primarily on boardroom decision making. A family fable is included. I have used this fable in focusing directors of business enterprise on the complexity of just one prong of ethical conduct—director's personal ethics.

Note that the term *morals* is usually reserved for persons and the term *ethics* is used for groups of persons, such as organizations, boards of directors, plus contextual ethics of an economic, social, or political system.

Dr. Verne Henderson has proposed one protocol for making choices when faced with an ethical dilemma. He illustrates the process with an Ethical IQ Test using true-life dilemmas from business.[2]

The ethical algorithm calls for a first-reaction answer to the case questions with a choice of no, depends, or yes. The answer should reflect what you believe you would actually do in the situation, not what you think you ought to do or believe is the best or most ethical answer.

Henderson's Ethical IQ Test rating system is an animating guide for assessing individual ethical decision-making patterns. A high preponderance in either the no, depends, or yes categories indicates you have a strong consistent sense of ethics. A formula for rating your responses by highest or lowest response category characterizes you either as a paragon of virtue, an indecisive person, or a person willing to make exceptions to the generally accepted norms or written rules of the game. The ethics test can also flush out the ethically alienated, the ethically confused, the purist, the expedient, and the pragmatist. Conduct your own ethics test by prescribing your own choices on the six anguished ethics cases.

ANCHORING POINTS FOR ETHICAL DECISION MAKING

Framing integrated ethics accountability. In a domain where neither law, regulation, nor traditionally well-delineated procedures dictate conduct, corporate directors must depend on their sense of ethical responsibility, intuition, and instinct to help cope with uncertainty. This is Moulton's domain of obedience to the unenforceable, referred to in the introductory section called "Moulton's Manners."

Greater board effectiveness requires forging closer links between personal values, organizational values, and external economic, social, and political values. When individual directors and the company have shared values, much of the uncertainty arising during decision making, conflict resolution, strategy development, and problem solving can be minimized.

It is questionable whether ethical responsibility can, or should be, institutionalized much beyond that inherent in legal doctrines. Such a goal assumes a common definition of ethics, such as: (1) a set of principles that prescribes a particular code of behavior; (2) discipline dealing with what is good and right, or bad and wrong; and (3) discipline concerned with personal moral duty and obligation.

Conventional definitions of ethics are too static. They presume that eternal verities or intrinsic values are always and everywhere the same. Examples in the business context are as follows:

- Competition is always desirable.
- Bigness is immoral.
- All corporations are predatory.
- Free enterprise must be constrained.
- Shareowners are victimized by management.
- Business is obligated to help society.
- Regulations are imperilling the effectiveness of corporations.
- Corporate law is the vehicle to deal with social problems.
- Consumer interests mandate further government intervention.
- General interest group representation on boards is correct.

A static definition of ethics presumes an inflexible relationship between governance principles and director behavior. Such inflexibility does not exist in the boardroom or in real life. The business environment is far more dynamic, turbulent, discontinuous, and uncertain than the static definition of ethics acknowledges. Society now expects more of corporations than economic utility.

A dynamic interpretation of ethics is that ethics are concerned with clarifying what constitutes human welfare and the kind of conduct necessary to promote it. This varies around the world.

In corporate governance, ethics implies a process of deliberation and debate on conduct necessary to promote human welfare. This continuing process of clarification is in response to new values, emerging technological and social developments, and shifting political forces.

One of the most important keys to greater board effectiveness is a closer link between personal and organizational values that are all within the values and conventions at the system level of international business practice.

EVOLUTION OF BUSINESS ETHICS IN A FIRM

An enterprise's overall philosophy or thrust toward applied ethics may be described in three evolutionary stages.

Stage 1 The company's efforts are characterized by the desire to stay out of trouble. The focus is on solving immediate and most recognized ethical problems. Here the ethical decision-making process tends to be nonformal. For the most part, responsibility lies with lawyers and managers who address only the necessary laws and regulations—constraints that leave no room for interpretation.

Stage 2   This stage involves governing and managing for compliance. The company builds a more formal system to govern and manage with the desired level and degree of literal compliance. This shift may stem from a company's desire to better govern and manage what is prescribed by the spirit of the law or company policies and by various regulatory requirements.

Stage 3   This stage, governing for ethical assurance, involves a basic governance and management philosophy covering the full range of potential ethical risks of the corporation's activities and impact on the environment and stakeholders. These risks must be governed and managed. Each case may vary.

Not only is there an ethical tone-at-the-top but the company's code of conduct is compliance related and ethical-assurance oriented. Also, all risks not yet covered by regulatory requirements or existing external standards must be considered in the decision-making process.

Three ethical foci nest dynamically within each other. They concern ethics from: (1) the personal-self standpoint, (2) ethics from the organizational or enterprise standpoint, and (3) ethics of the system in which the enterprise operates, such as the society as a whole. These foci have been referred to as the micro, macro, and meta levels of ethics.

As a group, directors of corporate boards face a double dilemma when it comes to questions of right or wrong: First, should they take action at all? Second, on whose behalf should they act?

Boards of directors take a position when they resolve or act on ethical dilemmas. They must choose the interests they represent very carefully. In taking these positions, the board should anticipate the consequences. Three that are most important: (1) What is the likely long-term versus short-term impact of the decision under consideration? (2) Which constituents will be most affected and what are their likely reactions? and (3) Is there an exogenous factor looming on the horizon?

FOUR PERSONAL QUESTIONS TO RESOLVE

Is it legal? Some professional advice may be necessary. Morality and legality are not always congruent. Different cultures may have different value systems and legal systems. The passage of the Foreign

Corrupt Practices Act in the United States raised this complex issue in the interpretations of ethical and legal behavior of American corporations operating in other world areas.

Higher ethical standards are in the domain of obedience to the unenforceable. Obedience to the law, in contrast, is enforceable. The law serves as a baseline of constraint for corporate or personal action. Its demands are relatively clear. Unfortunately, dynamic ethical issues are clearest in hindsight and they constitute a domain of uncertainty for individuals and for boards of directors.

Is it balanced? This concerns the undesirability principle which is similar to the uncertainty principle in physics. In physics, the product of uncertainties in two related quantities (e.g., the momentum of a particle and its position in space) is equal to or greater than a constant. In society, the product of uncertain costs of two or more conflicting courses of actions is a constant.

Therefore, society can obtain one goal to whatever degree of desirability it wishes provided it is willing to pay the price in loss of desirability of the other goals. When making the decision, is the gain worth any loss which might ensue?

What would I do if the matter appears in the next day's newspaper? How will it make me feel about myself, and how will it affect my family? This question concerns ethics viewed from the focus of a personal standpoint. It is one of the three ethical foci present in decision making. The other two foci are ethics of the organization and ethics of society.

A concluding statement for this chapter is: Wearing the trousers of decorum is a matter of business etiquette. However, as Peter Drucker notes, ethics stays in the prefaces of the average business-science books. Perhaps the time has arrived to fashion designer pants which are labeled "ethiquette" for vanguard, business-leader wardrobes?

8

A Director's Guide to Staying Clean: Spirit as Well as Letter of the Law

Nowhere is the confusion between legal and moral ideas more manifest than in the law of contract. Among other things, here again the so-called primary rights and duties are invested with a mystic significance beyond what can be assigned and explained.

The duty to keep a contract at common law means a prediction that you must pay damages if you do not keep it—and nothing else. If you commit a tort, you are liable to pay a compensatory sum. If you commit a contract, you are liable to pay a compensatory sum unless the promised event comes to pass, and that is all the difference.

But such a mode of looking at the matter stinks in the nostrils of those who think it advantageous to get as much ethics into the law as they can.

—Oliver Wendell Holmes, Jr. (1841–1935)
From *The Common Law* and the *Collected Legal Papers*

Those who have studied anthropology or sociology will recognize the sacred–profane theory of the great French sociologist, Emile Durkheim, concerning the social origins of religion.[1] Central to his ideas was the premise that all life experience can be indicated in a binary mode. Humans organize life's experience into the opposed categories of sacred and profane, the elegant or the mundane, the remarkable or the ordinary, or the noble or the base.

Durkheim went on to the more inclusive argument that the basic dualism of his sacred–profane theory was humanity's first and primary attempt at classification. It was the initial step toward the development of rationality. Having reason and understanding is an enviable attribute that effective directors can and should provide to an incorporated enterprise. For the contemporary director or trustee, we should add the binary mode of ethical and unethical—moral and immoral (or amoral).

Durkheim's idea was that human reason proceeds by organizing the world and experience into paired categories. Each element of the dyad is conceived of as opposite in meaning to the other. The notion dates back to the Greek philosophers and was carried into European thought by the early church fathers.

Normally, the ordinary or profane world can be handled in a pragmatic, linear, matter-of-fact way. It is nothing more than the here-and-now realm of everyday life. Many know this from business, government, or professional experience with their many contractual relationships.

Ordinary mortals can also deal with the sacred or remarkable, but only if they recognize certain nonlinear circumstances involving trust, ethical and moral insights, vision, inspiration, diplomacy, formality, sensitivity, attitudes, and care. These are vital to survival, development, and competitive positioning of any organization. These relationships are largely covenantal.

LAW AND MANNERS

The Guinness Book of Records reports that in March 1959 all the laws that were on the statute books of both federal and state governments totaled 1,156,644. Legal statisticians estimate that World War II and the depression almost doubled the number existent prior to those events. Perhaps the trend is uncontrollable. Contemporary experience would validate what Lao-Tse, founder of Taoism, observed in 604 BC: the greater the number of statutes, the greater the number of thieves and brigands. If stakeholders can't persuade corporations to trade-off some private corporate interests for public good, they will continue to get the government to do it. Boards of directors must see that the corporations they govern take responsible action to defuse or anticipate stakeholder irritation.

John Fiske (1842–1901), American historian and philosopher and a Harvard Law School graduate and brilliant university lecturer in philosophy, pointed out that "in a sinless and painless world, the moral element would be lacking; the goodness would have no more significance in our conscious life than that load of atmosphere which we are always carrying about us."[2] However, this load of atmosphere, including its codes of ethics and codes of corporate conduct, doesn't prevent directors from sinning, given the many statutes, regulations, or changes in the public's expectations and perceptions of proper corporate behavior. Such codes merely prevent directors from enjoying their sins to the same extent they might have in the good old days.

Social accountability—the notion of social accountability of the director as a fiduciary, a prudent person, or a trustee, and as an insider—has done the concept of directorship a great service by making such service a potential sin in many viewers' eyes. Being an effective director may be the best part of repentance. Every director's sin is the result of collaboration. Ovid said it properly in about 20 BC (before corporations): "If Jupiter hurled his thunderbolts as often as man sinned, he would soon be out of thunderbolts."

To avoid the modern equivalent of Jupiter's thunderbolts, there are some clean ways a director can conduct himself or herself. The following guides to behavior may let God forgive you for little wanderings or transgressions in board service, even if your nervous system won't.[3]

Guide One

Never use your board position to make a personal profit for yourself or someone else. In an unprecedented action in April 1982, the SEC had a Seattle accountant, Gary L. Martin, jailed until a $1.1 million profit he made with insider information was frozen. He made the profit by trading in Santa Fe International Corporation stock options soon after the Kuwait government announced it would purchase the oil company. Martin learned of the company takeover when he was a personal accountant of one of the company's directors. The director's loyalty to the corporation was indirectly in question because of his accountant's actions. The director's duty of loyalty did not apparently move him to oversee misuse of insider information for which he was responsible. The director, in this case, was not held personally responsible by the courts.

There is an interesting reversible-raincoat twist in the matter of the director's duty of loyalty to a corporation—a nonprofit corporation in this instance: "A director is a fiduciary; he cannot use his inside information or his strategic position for his own preferment. He cannot violate rules of fair play by doing indirectly through the corporation what he could not do directly." So said our Supreme Court in *Pepper* v *Litton* (308 U.S. 295 [1939]).

This interpretation didn't inhibit Jeffrey Ledowitz, chancellor and executive vice president of Embry-Riddle Aeronautical University. The school was founded in 1926 and now has over 6,000 students at campuses in Daytona Beach, Florida, and Prescott, Arizona. Some years ago, in a *Wall Street Journal* advertisement, the college offered membership on its board of trustees to anyone who donated $1 million to the school. Loyalty was not an explicit requirement. The chancellor defended this unusual recruiting device by saying that the university was merely stating publicly the same *quid pro quo* implied in the donor's relationships to other private colleges. The Reagan administration's reduction in federal student loans programs was cited as a precedent for this controversial seat-on-the-board offer. The National Association of Governing Boards of Universities and Colleges quickly criticized the plan, which put in question the criteria for trusteeship and model conduct of a corporation.

In another test of a director's loyalty to his corporation, I was a defendant at the United States District Court of New York in *Dolgow* v *Anderson* (43 FRD 21 [1967]). This was a class action suit brought by certain owners of Monsanto common stock alleging that officers, directors, and other insiders had deliberately misstated prospects of the company in order to drive up the price of its shares at a time when some of the individual defendants were selling their stock. The class action was prosecuted actively, appealed, and finally disallowed as not maintainable. The case was dismissed on merits and with prejudice in June 1972. Needless to say, my sensitivity to the vulnerability of a directorship position and the need for loyalty and exemplary behavior in matters of inside information were strongly branded in my mind just twenty-three years ago. The director's duty of loyalty is an absolute.

Guide Two

The "care" package that goes with board service is as important as the so-called duty of loyalty set forth in Guide One. It is called duty of care.

A key principle involved is the business judgment rule. This is essentially a defensive mechanism that insulates directors from hindsight review of their decisions. A director should perform in good faith in what is believed the best interests of the company and with the due care or diligence expected of a prudent person in like position.

The first big case associated with questionable foreign payment lawsuits introduced an ingenious and innovative interpretation of the business judgment rule. Corporations targeted in lawsuits established special committees of their directors to study whether the best interests of the corporation mandated a stockowners' derivative action against such parties. Such a litigation committee was created in the S.D.N.Y. in *Gall v Exxon Corporation* (418 F. Supp. 508 S.D.N.Y. [1976]). The derivative action sought $59 million from the directors for illegal payments made to Italian political parties and politicians from 1963 to 1979.

Out of this case, and many others, the business judgment rule evolved. It presupposes that directors are not in a conflict-of-interest situation, that a board enjoys a presumption of sound business judgment, and that its decisions will not be disturbed by a court if they can be attributed to any rational business purpose. Directors must be able to demonstrate that they in fact made a judgment. A paper trail of corporate minutes and other documents demonstrating that reasonable diligence and care have been exercised is very useful and perhaps essential to self-protection.

If a director performs his or her duties diligently, attends meetings regularly, and acts in good faith and with due care when making informed decisions, the business judgment rule is upheld as case law. Directors and managers, not the courts, best understand a corporation's need to nurture its business plans and work for the best interests of the corporation's diverse constituencies, most significantly all of its shareowners and employees. Back in 1903 in *Corbus v Alaska Treadwell Gold Mining Co.* (187 U.S. 455), the court wrote: "It is not a trifling thing for a stockholder to attempt to coerce the directors of a corporation to an act which their judgment does not approve, or to substitute his judgment for theirs."

The duty of due care essentially prohibits a director from neglecting his duties, mismanaging the corporation, exercising bad judgment, or intentionally causing the corporation to take illegal action.

Guide Three

Control of expenditures and transfers of corporate funds must be legitimate—no shell games with disbursements, no secret funds or secret bank accounts. This is primarily of concern to insiders or very inside outsiders.

Guide Four

Be sure of the accuracy of corporate disclosures. While directors have a duty to protect the confidentiality of information received, the statutes and regulations require certain disclosures of corporate and personal information that is relevant to the company's activities.

In the much-publicized, S.D.N.Y. case of *Escott* v *Bar-Chris Construction Corporation* (283 F. Supp. 643 S.D.N.Y. [1968]), directors who signed a registration statement for a securities offering were held liable under Section II of the Securities Act of 1933 for false and misleading statements about the business and financial condition of the issuer, which later went into bankruptcy. This case states in very clear terms that directors may not blindly rely on those who prepare a registration statement. After this case, the SEC amended its Form 10K, the annual report filed by companies registered with the commission, to require that the report be signed by at least a majority of the directors.

Since September 1982, the SEC has charged a number of companies with middle-management "book-cooking" during the recession, in the form of unorthodox and sometimes illegal bookkeeping practices. Allegedly these practices evolved as companies had been pressured by difficult production aims and economic problems. AM International, Inc., Saxon Industries Inc., McCormick & Co., Doughties Foods, Inc., and Ronson Corporation were so charged, with the Saxon and AM International cases allegedly including some complicity at corporate headquarters.

Guide Five

Be independent, informed, and objective. A strong group of independent directors on a board is a concept whose time has come. Board effectiveness was particularly improved during the period when Harold M. Williams served as chairman of the SEC from 1977 to 1981. Mr. Williams was an advocate of outside directors and campaigned strongly to increase the oversight responsibilities of corporate boards by competent outside (nonmanagement) directors, with a minimum of interlocking relationships with other corporations.

In a computer survey of 8,500 publicly held companies, compiled by Disclosure Inc., no person was found on more than eleven public boards, and only seventeen people were identified with eight or more directorships. The survey indicates that more outsiders are sitting on boards, which refutes the argument that inside directors—management, lawyers, and investment bankers serving the firm—dominate without truly objective, unaffiliated, and disinterested views.

The country-club, crony-dominated system of directorships is on the way out with publicly held companies. A University of Chicago Graduate School of Business study of seventy-five directors of large companies included interviews in which each director was presented with a list of forty randomly selected directors of Fortune 500 companies and asked to indicate how many of the directors he or she knew personally. One director spotted seven acquaintances but the rest knew on the average only one or two.

A clean director will think, speak, and act independently with confidence and courage. He or she will resist the tendency of a board to be a self-perpetuating protectorate unresponsive to change. Such a director is willing to risk social and peer rapport and back-scratching with the chairman, fellow directors, and the CEO if such must be sacrificed in order to take thoughtful, independent positions. The independent director would relinquish a directorship rather than be considered captive.

Guide Six

Stay away from political contribution or action unless the funds and the time involved are clearly your own, not the corporation's.

Guide Seven

Neither a director nor any member of his or her immediate family should accept or offer favors or gifts of goods, money, or services from or to competitors, suppliers, customers, or anyone who does business with the company on whose board he or she serves. Commonsense judgment is to be used on token gifts, nonmonetary courtesies, or hospitality in connection with performing company business. The problem is that acceptance can suggest that an improper business relationship exists.

The greatest domain of human action in the boardroom is the domain of manners, or obedience to the unenforceable, as cited by

Lord John Fletcher Moulton, a high official in the British Munitions Ministry in World War I (see Preface). This domain is different from the domain of positive law or the domain of free choice. The domain of obedience to the unenforceable is the sphere where we do what we should do though we are not obliged to do so by law.

Guide Eight

Obedience to the unenforceable is the subject of this book. Directors must do what their sense of fairness, ethics, values, beliefs, and personal integrity tell them, even though they may not be obliged to do so by law, regulation, or custom. Neither law, regulation, nor free choice is controlling. Conscience, beliefs, morals, personal attitudes, and ethics must dominate. In board deliberations, ethics are concerned with clarifying what constitutes human welfare and the kind of conduct necessary to promote it.

A corporate director's code of ethics is indeed puzzling. The board will dismiss a CEO when a merger of two companies takes place, but the chairman would regard it as an unforgivable breach of honor to take the CEO's last cigarette. Such is the difference between corporate ethics and personal ethics.

Some years ago the St. Louis brokerage firm of Stix & Co. collapsed as a result of a stock scam by James J. Massa, an Illinois attorney, and Duane Skinner, a certified public accountant from Illinois. Both were found guilty by a federal jury of conspiring in a stock scam; the charges against them included tax evasion, mail fraud, and obstruction of justice. Stix went into receivership after Massa took control in 1979, and company officers allegedly stole at least $36 million in securities from their clients' accounts. According to the charges, the fraud was brought about through false statements to clients, laundered money, falsified tax returns, and bogus securities.

A director who serves a financial institution has some special problems of "a higher duty of performance and behavior that is expected of him than of his business corporation peer," according to the courts.

Bank directors take an oath of office, have residency and citizenship requirements, have restrictions on the types of other boards on which they can serve as directors, and live with criminal laws which expressly prohibit certain acts by bankers, including embezzlement, making false entries, taking fees for loans, falsifying certifying checks, making or granting a loan or gratuity to a bank examiner, and borrowing funds entrusted to a bank under its trust powers.

No such direct targeting of criminal laws confronts the business corporation director.

In *Gamble* v *Brown* (299 F.2d 366 [1928]), bank directors were held liable for failure to appoint an audit committee, as required by by-laws, to discover that a vice president regularly made fictitious statements as to amounts in hands of other banks for collection, to check excessive and improvident loans made by the president, and to prevent him from making further loans. The SEC mandated in 1978 that each domestic company with common stock listed on the New York Stock Exchange establish an audit committee comprised solely of directors who are independent of management.

The comptroller of the currency succeeded in imposing personal liability on the directors of a national bank who had knowingly allowed the bank to exceed its legal lending limits by $350,000. The court ruled in *Del Junco* v *Conover* (682 F. 2nd 1338 [1982]), "Directors of a national bank operate in an area closely regulated by federal law, and cannot maintain ignorance of the law as a defense."

These guides to staying clean are only the tip of the iceberg of corporate governance. They are by no means the ten commandments. There are numerous other guide points in the complicated and dynamic domain of responsible corporate conduct. The corporation's legal counsel should take a lead role in advising the executive management and corporate directors on the legislative, regulatory trends, and case law decisions that are pertinent to the company's current and future business affairs. However, in the end, the individual director and the board must decide on the normative issue of what ought to be done.

The three concepts, the right, the good, and the fitting, are decisive for business ethics. No collection of simple guides will be adequate. Ethics is about how to live responsibly in general, and professional responsibility is about how we ought to live when we are doing business.

THE JOYS OF BEING A DIRECTOR[4]

The worry list of issues challenging multinational corporations is scary. It can include acute industrial crisis prevention and management, environmental assurance, takeover defense, merger damage control, industry and corporate restructuring, devastating global competition, deregulation, surprise technological shifts, social reforms, political upsets, terrorism, and so on.

Given this list of issues and the attack on board performance and pressures on some individuals to keep clean, there is a failure by many journalists, the government, lawyers, activists, academics, and some business leaders themselves to consider directorship's good side and the potential for improvement and achievements in the boardroom. Boardworthiness is worthwhile to the individual director and necessary for the enterprise.

Lest we cast all those accepting election to a board as not knowing enough about the liabilities and stress to be qualified to serve, let's quietly reflect on the joys of being a director, of which there are many despite the demise of the pleasurable, if passive, ceremonial board service of the past. Such reflection should elevate the spirit of individual directors as they obey not only the letter of the law but the unenforceable tenets of good manners and conduct as behavior becoming directorship.

Exhilaration of Challenge

Directors tackle vexing issues in their stewardship of owners' and public interest. They do this with thoughtful enthusiasm, and experience the thrill derived from surviving a risky experience or in chancing adventuresome deeds.

Most of us derive satisfaction out of challenges faced and resolved—the market share is always lower than you think; the number of competitors never declines; strategies develop most easily from big backlogs; any time things appear to be going smoothly, you don't have the right information; no matter how much of a dividend is declared, or how significant an acquisition or merger, some of the shareowners won't like it!

The exhilaration of gaming to overcome these challenges and conflicts is ever present in the boardroom. This motivates many to seek directorships even though the peer power is fierce and the liabilities are increasing. In *The Lady of the Lake*, Sir Walter Scott called this exhilaration reaction, "The stern joy which warriors feel in foeman worthy of their steel."

The Service Ethic

Most of us are initially driven by the ethic of competition. As I get older and know more answers, I find that fewer people ask me. But I do get a bigger charge out of the ethic of service. This is not the mowing your neighbor's lawn-type ethic. This is an enlightened brand of altruism in the boardroom which never misses an opportunity to make the stakeholders happy, even if you have to leave them alone to do so. While private ethical values inevitably affect corporate decisions, a corporate code of ethics is helpful to guide voluntary assumption of self-discipline above and beyond the requirements of the law.

Wisdom in board affairs is knowing what's right to do next. Skill is knowing how to do it. Virtue is in not doing it yourself but seeing that the company does it. Directors, as nonexecutive stewards, learn to use fly swatters, not sledgehammers, in offering advice and service to a corporation.

Eliteness Motivation

Someone once opined that the only purpose of a board of directors is to exclude others from membership. While that may be cynical, it's no good being elite unless the people you know perceive how elite you are. There is a consistent eliteness pattern of identification with and of membership in prestigious organizations. Upward mobility forces a positive striving to achieve these elite, dignified associations.

In a social sense, boards have far-reaching powers. By their approval or disapproval, they direct the flow of capital. They start new industries or businesses which sometimes drive out old ones. Rubbing shoulders with people you admire promotes the upward pressure to achieve. The more mundane but important matters of cultural and educational background, personal style, personality, dress, manners, poise, and general state of maturity are also engaging elements of an elite cadre of directors.

The Ethical Algorithm

Ethics are commonly considered a set of principles, eternal verities, or intrinsic values. Ethics prescribe a code of behavior or represent a discipline dealing with what is good and right and what is bad, wrong, or immoral. The reality of ethical conduct in a boardroom is not static. The attraction for a director is the role he or she can play in clarifying what constitutes human welfare and the kind of corporate conduct that can be instituted to promote such welfare.

Ethics in corporate governance is an illuminating experience. It implies a process of deliberation and debate among fellow directors who share concerns for the social consequences and fabric. This is a continuous, case-by-case, intellectual and emotional process of clarification. It must respond to new values, emerging technological and social developments, or shifting internal and external political forces. There is an ethical logic system in approaching vexatious matters, and it can be gratifying to participate in such a process. Chapter 7 offers a protocol for choices in ethical decision making through use of an ethical algorithm.

Ethics has a much larger role in the boardroom than supplying decisions or procedures or in offering some formal normative orientation. An ethical algorithm or pattern of steps becomes a form of the art of directorship, giving credibility to the governance process and also to the art of managing. Great satisfaction can be derived from being a part of this dynamic.

The Celebrity Role

I am reminded of the upwardly mobile executive who was asked by a program committee about his speaker's fee. He said his fee was $100, but to appear before some groups he'd pay $200. Many would-be directors yearn for the implied celebrity status of board election. Some would even pay to get into a directors' celebrity class.

There is joy in becoming recognized as a director of a well-known corporation. You can then be whisked from airport to boardroom in a Cadillac with tinted windows so that no one will know who you are! There are some days in the boardroom when it takes all you've got just to keep up with the losers and the lawsuits. If you're not notable yourself, it's a pleasure to sit on a board with one or more persons who are. Something may rub off, and it gives you an opportunity to do some restrained name-dropping at cocktail parties.

Do not forget the cascade effect of being on a distinguished board. "Oh, tell us the marvelous exploits you did to deserve those medals," a general whose chest was covered with medals was asked. "I got the small bronze one by mistake," he replied. "The silver one next to it came because I had the bronze, and so on." Invitations to multiple directorships can be accreted by the cascade effect.

The Ego Factor

An ego is one of the few elements of directorship that can grow without nourishment. It is either a measure of the importance with which a person holds himself or it can be a form of self-confidence searching for trouble. Psychologists emphasize that each of us is constantly making choices, great and small, which cumulatively determine the kind of person we become. This drive is concerned with our attempts to discover the satisfying sense of personal identity and to give meaning to our lives. At a Boston Bar Association meeting in March 1900, Oliver Wendell Holmes, Jr., put it this way: "The joy of life is to put one's power in some natural and useful or harmless way. There is no other. And the real misery is not to do this." Making it to the boardroom is one manifestation of the ego factor.

The Marching and Chowder Society

We all like parades, parties, and performances. Going through the usual boardroom drill is rewarding and some enjoy the ritualistic and ceremonial aspects. While the passive ceremonial board is fast becoming an endangered species in these litigious days, there still is psychic reward to be gained from performing in a boardroom or in a preprandial gathering of directors. Social networking benefits of board membership can be a joy to have and to hold as we experience such festivity.

Before I became a chairman, I had a dozen theories about how a board should work. Then I chaired a dozen directors but had no good theory, except to observe that the marching and chowder society aspects of board affairs can be enjoyable. Emeritus directors, especially, enjoy the social climate of board meetings. They always attend, regardless of the weather or agenda.

Team Play

Peer acceptance on a board team gives many of us a social contract with interesting people that we would otherwise not have a chance to work with or even meet. Membership on a successful, active board can indeed be a joy. It's particularly rewarding to compare your own judgments, beliefs, values, articles of faith, sense of ethics, and propriety of conduct with thoughtful, responsible fellow directors. Most of us enjoy such group participation.

Networking

Old boy, and now old girl, networks have long been associated with directorship. Networks are effective channels of communication, influence, and power and are important components of corporate achievement. The access to outside networks afforded by nonexecutive directors can be a valuable resource for identifying trends, opportunities, and challenges in the environment.

Belonging to a board puts you into the crosshatched matrix of other directors' networks. Where appropriate, you can connect and offer your own personal and business networks to other directors. This can be a meaningful exchange of trust, contacts, and communications. One of the things I truly enjoy on boards of directors is the opportunity to add to my own networks and to offer them to others who may find my networking contacts helpful. As someone once said, "A network is a club without premises, constitution, or life membership; not simply a clique, not quite an elite, not exactly a trade union but some of the qualities of all these alliances."

Perks and Pay

The pay for giving advice and being accountable in a boardroom can be significant. There are three types of compensation for a director, namely, real income, psychic income, and perquisites. The fees are governed by competitive ranges which are, in part, a function of meeting frequency, and not often a result of director effectiveness. The issue of appropriate fees is a hot one in the 1990s.

The IRS notwithstanding, perks can be rewarding, sometimes even a thing of beauty and a joy forever. Examples of perks may include: charitable matching-gift programs; club and association memberships; company chauffeuring at board functions; spouse inclusion in occasional social gatherings; director benefit plans such as stock options, pensions, and insurance entertainment before or after board meetings; executive aircraft travel privileges; medical benefits, office space and services; special travel excursions to pleasant meeting spots or facility visits; and memorabilia and mementos. These are among the more familiar forms of perquisite used as director compensation.

While such perks may give a hedonic tone to boardroom service, they are actually the least enduring and satisfying joys of directorship. The real reward of serving on an effective board is in the service-without-dominance ethic and the exultant challenge of governing in risky circumstances with a select group of respected peers. Dostoevsky expressed the thinking better on this perspective of corporate governance: "Man is fond of counting his troubles, but he does not count his joys. If he counted them up as he ought to, he would see that every lot has enough happiness provided for it."

9

Smart Directorship: Knowledge and Judgment

But when the objective is critical thinking (in the liberal arts setting, for example) or problem-solving (in the professional school milieu), and the development of qualities such as sensitivity, cooperation, and zest for discovery, discussion pedagogy offers substantial advantages.

—C. Roland Christensen
Robert Walmsley University Professor Emeritus
Harvard University[1]

Chris, as he is respectfully known by his students, colleagues, fellow corporate board members and friends, defined *discussion teaching* as a systematic way of constructing a context for learning from the knowledge and experience of students, rather than exclusively from the canons of disciplinary knowledge. The lessons are those of case study teaching.

The process is particularly suitable for corporate director learning when the board engages in a director development and renewal effort. An increasing number of corporations are taking advantage of seminars, workshops, conferences, and other educational programs offered by universities, professional associations, and consulting firms. These learning experiences focus on improving effectiveness of enterprise governance. The thrust is to assist directors in addressing the changing role of the board given the current attention focused on boardworthiness.

Another important insight from current research on human learning is that the acquisition and application of knowledge are fundamental acts. Professor Christensen and his fellow authors focused on new literature for teaching that captures the wisdom of practice. Their book, *Education for Judgement* (1991), fills a teaching resource need in most every educational program—schoolrooms and, I submit, modern-day boardrooms.

This concept happens to be a significant anchoring point for our topic of corporate director orientation and continuing board development. Historically, institutions have paid more attention to executive management training and development than most of them devote to their own board director orientation and board development. The artistry of directorship is a deep, complex, layered challenge which yields answers in the form of new questions. A key issue is uncertainty. Some continuing education is in order for enhancing knowledge and judgment.

THE UNCERTAINTY OF DIRECTORSHIP

Teaching has been described as a messy, indeterminate, inscrutable, often intimidating, and highly uncertain task. Corporate directorship is also a vexatious, individual challenge to directors, would-be directors, board chairmen, and CEOs. The primary concern is the uncertainty of conditions surrounding the enterprise and the issues or decisions before the board. One perennial challenge of enterprise governance is seeking ways to govern effectively in the face of such uncertainty by reducing as much of it as possible to a measurable portfolio of business risks.

Directors implicitly search for patterns. There are some general patterns which connect and show either a step function, feedback loops, slow change, accelerating change, stabilization, emergence, peaks, discontinuities, gaps, repressions, chaotic trajectories, or novelties— all buzzwords of management scientists and business schools. Given the patterns, attention is turned to the governance process.

The process is discovering what uncertainties can be converted to manageable risk. This is normally a primary task of the executive management for judgment and decisions by the board.

There are important distinctions between certainty, risk, and uncertainty. Risk, where the probabilities of events or courses are known, is a special case of uncertainty. The set of risk variables that a director must deal with may be viewed as a continuum from complete determination on one end to the complete unknown situation at the other end. In our space age, scientists refer to this extreme as "unk-unks," or unknown-unknowns. Unfortunately, the scope of board action is greatest when our knowledge is the least complete. The scope of board action is the least when the scope of the directors' knowledge is the greatest.

One interesting technique used in strategic thinking regarding the murky view of the uncertain future is the use of alternative futures scenarios. In a recent study by Arthur D. Little, Inc., for a large multinational financial institution, we characterized two dominant driving forces of primary interest to the U.S.-based firm. The first was the relative level of world interactivity. The second was the character of U.S. government intervention in the private sector.

Alternative scenarios were developed given the present world condition, with increasing intensity of international interactions. For example, major trading nations would develop more multilateral tariff and nontariff arrangements to facilitate trade and investment. New international monetary and judicial systems would evolve, as would international codes of conduct under such a scenario of events.

Alternatively, if a protectionist scenario evolved in the 1990s with a lower global level of interaction, breakdown of some international institutions such as the International Monetary Fund (IMF) could be threatened. Such an autarkic world is inherently one of recession or depression, with currency instability, trade restrictions, and quotas. Internal industries would be restructured to reduce reliance on outsiders. Investment flows would weaken and trade barriers would rise as each nation attempted to follow a policy of self-sufficiency.

Another alternative could evolve by a move toward a more privatized form of government interaction, similar to that in Japan and Holland or to the more bureaucratic form experienced in the United States during Depression years or after World War II.

Using these alternative scenarios, some of the uncertainties could be hypothesized as determined states or forecast conditions. In other words, they could be reduced to probalistic risk situations for the purposes of thinking through the consequences. In this study, we identified 123 separate global trends and shifts, including twenty-four areas of technological change which could affect industries served by the company.

These trends and shifts were grouped as social-cultural, regulatory, techno-economic, and international trend clusters. Eight of the broader movements called for new thinking at the multinational company board level and new abilities at the executive level. The client made a complete overhaul of its management development plans in order to develop managers for the future who will be capable of managing a wide range of probable conditions. Interestingly, the client company did not include any specific, developmental and educational plan for members of its board of directors. Undoubtedly, this will come later.

DEVELOPMENT OF CLINICAL JUDGMENT

Smart directorship translates into knowledge and judgment. How to insure that a corporation has a board of directors with each member competent in making effective clinical business judgments is a topic of increasing attention. Other organizations study special problems by concrete examples and expert advice or treatment given, as in a vocational clinic.

Legislators, regulators, institutional investors, shareowner and environmental activists, academic researchers, vanguard business leaders, investment analysts, journalists, business ethicists, and the general public are focusing on the mutating role of the board and effective performance of individual directors. Publicly traded companies are becoming more sensitive to criteria of competence, knowledge, accountability, independence, and integrity in their boardrooms.

The development of clinical-type judgment, the formation of critical skills, and the shaping of covenantal sensibility in directorship are not popular topics for lectures to corporate directors. Neither is the process of director orientation and subsequent development if the effort is primarily devoted to information transfer. Few directors like or welcome lectures as part of their fiduciary, oversight role.

Alternate models need to be employed for director learning and development. In the classroom context, inappropriate for the boardroom, the core concept is teaching. For boards of directors, the core concept is self-directed learning with an appropriate venue, timing, format, and circumstance. Such mutual learning experiences should have a clear relationship to individual director's contributions and level of involvement.

John Dewey, American philosopher and educator, pointed out the absurdity of the teacher-centered approach to education over six decades ago. He wrote "Teaching can be compared to selling commodities. No one can sell unless someone buys . . . (yet) there are teachers who think they have done a good day's teaching irrespective of what pupils have learned."[2]

THE STEINZOR EFFECT ON BOARDROOM BEHAVIOR[3]

Starting in the 1950s, behavioral scientists began to discover conditions which enhanced the effectiveness of groups as problem-solving and decision-making entities. These findings apply to many current boardroom situations. The first major effort to investigate the impact of spatial arrangements was carried out by Dr. Steinzor, and his findings are referred to as the Steinzor Effect (1950).

Another investigator found that members of discussion groups with passive leaders directed more comments to persons sitting opposite them than to those on either side of them. With a strong directive leader, members tended to interact more with their neighbors than with those sitting across from them. This suggests that leadership style has a significant influence on the impact of spatial arrangement in developing interpersonal communication patterns within groups.

Manifestation of the Steinzor Effect depends on the degree of direction given by the designated leader. The greater the formal designation of leadership, the less the tendency for the Steinzor Effect to appear. It's not that the chairman is more intelligent than you; he just appears more convincing.

In a study of 467 participants in an officers' training program, observers found that persons sitting at the end position of the table rated significantly higher on the leadership scale than persons in middle positions. Study of a twelve-man jury seated at rectangular tables showed that jurors who seated themselves in end positions participated more and were perceived as having more influence on the jury's decision than persons sitting in middle positions. Steinzor concluded that the mean sitting distance is the determination of leadership emergence within a group. Check this out the next time you're in a board meeting. I've found this effect to be true on many occasions.

Spatial position also determines the flow of communication which in turn determines leadership emergence. At a five-person, decision-making group seated at a rectangular table, with three persons on one side and two on the opposite side, the two-person side greatly influenced the three persons on the other side. As predicted, members of the two-person side were shown to emerge more frequently as leaders than members of the three-person side. The rule that says, Never arrive on time to avoid being classed as a beginner, also prevails.

With respect to interpersonal relations, when the group size increases above three persons there is a tendency for the leader to assume a position at the end of the table. In such cases, the other group members normally sit as close as possible to the leader. Only rarely is the chair at the end opposite the leader used. Boardroom seating often reserves the seats adjacent to the chairman for senior directors, those who have not reached the statutory senility of by-law retirement age.

The Steinzor Effect and other studies have certain administrative implications for designing and participating in decision-making groups. Boardroom architecture and director dynamics are obvious implications. Several other implications seem to be useful as a focus for the chairman of the board to target and model his directorate. Trade-offs have to be made to get the optimal arrangement for the board situation. The size of the firm and nature of its business or businesses influence the board size. The following are useful administrative implications:

- Since the quality of board decisions is of major importance, it is useful to have a larger number of board members, say seven to twelve, so that more inputs are available to the board in making its decisions.

- A board of this size functions more effectively with a designated leader. This has recently been recommended by notable corporate governance scholars and experienced chairmen and CEOs. (Note: Some boards do not have chairmen.) The chairman should be seated at the head of the table or at the end of the room. In less formal gatherings, such as committees, the most acceptable leader can often be identified by seating all members equidistant from one another, such as around a circular table, and then observing the member to whom most of the useful comments are directed. This person is usually a most likely candidate for chairman.

- If degree of consensus is of primary importance, it is useful to choose a smaller group (three to five) so that each board member can have his or her concern considered and discussed. Airtime is at a premium.

- Director's satisfaction and time to reach agreement are found to be favorably managed by using smaller groups. Remember that committees or boards with three members often cause one member to have low satisfaction. On the other hand, boards with four members often have high conflict and thus may not reach a quick consensus.

- Group conflict is known to be greatest on even-number boards. Ideally, a chairman should use committees of five to seven with simultaneous recognition of the need for diverse inputs and provision for coordination and control with the larger board.

- Spatial arrangements can be used to minimize conflict. Board or committee members who anticipate being antagonistic tend to sit across from one another. Members who sit across from one another also tend to have frequent and argumentative communications. A useful strategy for the chairman is to seat members with a high conflict potential beside one another. If there are two subgroups of high conflict potential, consider using alternate seating for the members.

Before suggesting some anchoring points for board of director orientation and development programming, assuming that such is needed, welcomed, and appropriately arranged, an obvious operational component is indicated.

THE BOARD INFORMATION SYSTEM

The board's information system is the core of any smart meeting or programmed learning, either in formal statutory meetings, adjunct-type director-executive management meetings, informal retreat gatherings, special events, and inspection or facility visitations and excursions. Information transfer for these occasions is a core process whether the board is being hosted, entertained, or gathered for networking, community building, a learning experience, or social purposes.

An information system for smart meeting and development programming should be a built-in, continuous, and supportive process. It provides board members with significant information about conduct of the corporation and its extended affairs. In general, the information should do the following:

- Be adequate and free-flowing before and during meetings in order to make any gathering meaningful. This requires providing financial, policy, other relevant reports, and detailed agendas in advance to board members. Normally, the board chairperson and the chief executive draw up the program.

- Permit the board to use the relevant information efficiently in conducting its affairs. This outcome requires good chairing to keep discussion on track and to appropriate the time to significant matters.

- Eliminate extraneous detail so that essential facts and observations become available to participants. Usually, it is best to provide information as homework well before any meeting. This could include a clear summary of policy matters, important features, and any recommendations from the executive director and board committee chairs when such is indicated.

- Be relevant to the purpose and objectives of the specific meeting's programmed deliberations. This requires the chairperson to guide the meeting carefully, permitting all points of view to be aired. A meeting involving decision making is obviously programmed differently from an informative session, a sharing and interchange of director experience, a consciousness-raising event, a role-playing exercise, a case study, a brain-storming workshop, a focus-group assignment, and a conventional social affair or celebration.

- Enable the board to achieve its meeting purposes. The chairperson should move the board to closure on as many agenda items as possible if the meeting is for the purpose of specific decision making. This may require discussion-teaching (case study) experience and some training in development with the chief executive and key board members. It may also require a suitable process strategy for the meeting, including tactics to help members come to closure, reaching desirable policy conclusions, or may be rewarded with meaningful information exchange and a learning experience.

MASTERY OF PROCESS AND CONTENT

Coping with uncertainty, development of clinical judgment, and having an effective board information system and process as part of the governance-management covenantal culture are key features of smart directorship. They are prerequisites to the dual competency of mastering process and content of candid exchange of attitudes and shared experiences, provoking critical thinking, and of receptive exposure to outside experts on trends, new governance insights, or concepts. Further, smart directorship can enhance the role of the board and offer psychic rewards for being a director.

The notion of dual instructional competency involves dual preparation by the discussion leader and the individual director. The leader of a board-learning session can develop his or her own approach to staging an effective event.

To develop an approach, have clear profiles in mind of the board as a group and of its individual members. This means sizing up their experience, any distinguished career achievements, education, attitudes, value systems, relationships with other independent board members, personal networks, contributions as a director, and any biases, prejudices, or special interests.

Then, size up each director's intellectual and social strengths, any weaknesses, and his or her ability and willingness to contribute to the discussion process.

Consider whether the individual possesses the basic ideology and understanding of free-enterprise, corporate governance concepts and the statutory and regulatory requirements. This includes comprehending the covenantal relationships as distinct from contractual relationships involved.

After these steps, thoughtfully review the boardworthiness of each director. A do-it-yourself checkup has been proposed as one guide in this respect (see Appendix A).[4] The sixfold evaluative criteria are the following:

1. Commitment and interest of the individual director
2. Capacity and competence of the director as related to the needs of the corporation
3. Availability of the director for counsel and committee work
4. The directors' nonconflicting bridges and networks to allied sectors

5. General functional strength of the individual director

6. The director's role as a change agent

For the next step, informally evaluate individual director participants as to whether, in your opinion, he or she would have an honors, pass, or fail rating under objective peer review. Participants can be evaluated in the following areas:

1. Competence as director

2. Applied ethics

3. Independence

4. Social and environmental consciousness

5. Preparedness as director

6. Practice as director

7. Committee activity

8. Development process of the corporate enterprise

9. Ambassadorship

10. Attendance

11. Hierarchy of personal needs satisfaction

12. Chairman of the board as an agent of the board. Consider who is the responsible leader, the effective leader, or the psychological leader of the group? Recent thinking has focused on the importance of an independent, outside director assuming such a leadership role to better focus the impact of independent, nonexecutive, directors of a board of directors.

13. Special service directors. This is a selective criterion for an individual with exemplary contribution to the board in an expert professional role, perhaps as an apropos celebrity role or as a controlling shareowner's representative.

The hierarchy of personal needs criterion, listed as number 11, requires thoughtful consideration by the leader of a director's meeting which is devoted to improving effectiveness of the corporate governance setup. The challenge is to stimulate an exchange of experiences and ideas for the benefit of the enterprise and the individual participants, for example, an instructional learning experience devoted to the board's needs and an individual director's personal needs. This challenge warrants further comment.

BOARDWORTHINESS: PERSONAL NEEDS CRITERION

Maslow's positive theory of human motivation applies to directorship service in three of five salient needs. The first two personal needs, physiological and safety needs, are satisfied before nomination and election to a board.

For a director to qualify for honors, the challenge and rewards of board service should be satisfying in all three of the higher needs: belonging needs (sociability, acceptance); esteem needs (status, prestige, acknowledgement); and the highest need, self-actualization (personal fulfillment and growth).

The director would view directorship as an ethical service. Service on the board is seen as an effective way society devised to balance the ethic of competition with the ethic of service to the owners and stakeholders of a corporate enterprise. He or she strives to improve public trust and confidence in the corporation and its board members by exemplary personal conduct, while fulfilling the role of a director, serving in a worthy, prestigious position.

The director assists the corporation to achieve vanguard status regarding long-term perspective of distinguished corporate conduct. Vanguard companies are those seeking to serve stakeholder interests rather than being obsessed only with profits. Research shows vanguard companies are more profitable in the long run.

The honors director enjoys the exhilaration and challenge in tackling vexatious issues as steward of owners' and stakeholders' interests. He or she receives gratification from the recognition of serving effectively on a competent board of a reputable, progressive enterprise. By their approval or disapproval, boards direct the flow of capital, both financial and human. Board decisions often start new businesses or industries and provide gratification to those wielding board power.

The honors director is a team player. The extension and empowerment of directors' external networks can be beneficial for the enterprise and psychically rewarding for the individual director.

Finally, the honors director receives personal fulfillment by taking part (with a select group of respected peers) in the board learning process and in governing an enterprise under risky, uncertain circumstances.

Quality and Quantity[5]

Sir E. Roy Griffiths is known throughout the world as the author of *The Griffiths Report*, a report written in 1983 that revolutionized British health care. And while he is most renowned for his work with that country's National Health Service, it was his management and boardroom experience with J. Sainsbury, the U.K.'s most prestigious retail food-store enterprise, that prepared him for public service and led to the knighthood that followed. Sir Roy was a long-time personal friend who, tragically, became ill and died last year.

Sainsbury was a year away from celebrating its centennial when Griffiths joined the 100-percent family-owned business in 1968. The company was enormously well regarded nationally and had 30 percent of the food trade in the London area. Griffiths was the first person to come in from the outside and go directly onto the board. While his title was director of personnel, his mandate was to change management style from a mid-sized, family-owned enterprise to a much larger, publicly held entity driven by the same traditional values that had already given it such a strong market share.

In a family-dominated business, there are traditionally two styles of operation: the family system and the business system. The family system protects values; the business system looks to the bottom line. According to Griffiths, he bridged them both, maintaining "a third-party, objective relationship with both the family and the nonfamily people in the company."

He cites the addition of professionalism as his primary recruitment attribute—professionalism that would enhance the company's operating efficiency while also taking advantage of its legacy of quality. Explains Griffiths, "It surprised me that profitability was something that nobody got particularly excited about. If you wanted excitement in a big way—an explosion—it happened when a store reported back that the goods it had been displaying were 'out of code'—if their 'sell by' date had lapsed. Or if a director had walked into a store and found the customer service was poor or the availability of merchandise was not what it should be. I really do believe that one of the hallmarks that made this company great is an overriding obsession with quality."

In an increasingly competitive marketplace, such an obsession, however, was just the kind of tender spot that could inhibit growth. Griffiths added to this a concern for profitability.

As Griffiths oversaw the natural business evolution of the company, he learned some things. He says, "If you are running an organization, you are concerned with three things. One is the quality of product or service. Second is productivity and efficiency. The third is the motivation of people to achieve the first two things."

To insure the survival of all three while adding beef to Sainsburys' bottom line, Griffith embraced the concept of board partnership as he oversaw the natural business evolution of the company. A public offering took place in 1973. Two years later, the board was more properly balanced between three family members and thirteen nonfamily directors. Outside directors made their first board appearance in 1980. Griffith had lost none of the implicit passion for excellence that had so dignified the family operation.

The issue of motivation can be a delicate one for directors whose service tends to be based on intelligence and experience rather than on zeal and exuberance. Sainsbury asks its board members to work hard but not foolishly, as personal balance is as much a part of the corporate culture as professional equilibrium. Griffiths explains, "It has been a very beneficial feature of working at Sainsburys that you have to give a lot of commitment to the company, but never twenty-four hours a day. Never. You could walk out of Sainsburys and get back to your own life, your family life, your social life. That was fine. That was as it should be."

When he started working with Sainsbury nearly a quarter-century ago, "profit was not the target, it was the result. If you wanted to set priorities, there was still the obsession with the company, its trading standards, and its level of customer service. One of our great successes was that we took that tremendous reputation and welded on to it a management process that enabled us to control costs, to gain greater efficiency, and to target profitability."

The unspoken rules of board conduct, therefore, allowed for sophisticated, modern-business strategic planning to flourish in a family culture. And not only was that combination a legacy on paper, it was a piece of heritage the directors worked hard to keep alive. Says Griffiths, "Among the seven directors who habitually went around to the stores, they totaled about 600 visits a year. That meant that each director was making, on average, eighty to ninety visits a year, which means one or two a week. It would be absolutely characteristic that an executive director was so thoroughly concerned with the store operations. That includes the chairman and the managing director spending one day a week out in the field."

How did outside directors, especially the nonexecutive, nonemployee people who signed on in the 1980s, keep up to snuff on the visitation program? "With difficulty," answers Griffiths, "but they were expected to make the trips. In their case, it was for a different purpose: to keep themselves up to date.

"Keeping up to date," he continues, is important because "outside directors are even more prone to the great danger of top people in the company being endlessly fooled by sitting behind the desk and looking at reports. As a managing director or chief executive, even your own colleagues want to tell you only what you want to hear. You really do have to go out and see whether the reports being brought to you are fiction or nonfiction."

Ignorance Is No Excuse

Sir Roy Griffiths had a wide range of tools before him to make his partnership with the board powerful enough to actually reshape a marketplace leader. For comparison, let me tell you about Charlie and the risk of not-so-smart directorship.

Charlie had many of the same tools of Sir Roy but chose to use none of them. Because he was unable to fully differentiate between fact and fiction, he didn't understand the tender spots in the business partnership between his office and his board of directors. The result was that he put his company at full exposure.

Charlie was the chief executive of a medium-sized electronics conglomerate whom I knew through our association as fellow board members of a financial intermediary company. A stolid, mature sort, Charlie had quietly but effectively overseen the growth of his company as it acquired an electric parts firm and brought it into his parent company as a wholly owned subsidiary. It was a strong, independent, entrepreneurial act and the performance earned him salutes from his competitors, encouragement from his colleagues, and regular rewards from his board.

The electric parts company remained a legal subsidiary but functioned as an operating division, a common enough practice in large multinational organizations. And while he didn't have the time to pay much attention to day-to-day activity once the acquisition had been made, Charlie was in charge, both as chairman of the parent and the new acquisition. He never asked for the support of either board because he felt he didn't need it. In truth, Charlie simply went on about the business of preparing for his next conquest.

It was shortly after the purchase that the entire senior management team of the equipment parts firm was found guilty of price-fixing practices, behavior that had preceded the acquisition and continued under the new ownership. There was more than just surprise for Charlie. There was legal accountability in the acquired firm, even though he was unaware of its improper behavior.

Charlie was sentenced to six months in jail, even though his only wrong had been not paying as close attention to the acquisition as he should have. He resigned in shame from his own company and from the board on which we had jointly sat.

I particularly remember the time I ran across Charlie at Logan Airport. He was in work clothes but carried no briefcase or business papers. His only possession was the duffel bag he was bringing to the prison in the South where he would spend the next six months. His wife and daughter had dropped him off at the airport, he told me, and he was on his way to one of the country club confinements. We tried to chat, but neither of us had a great deal to say.

Charlie served his term and returned home. He was never able to enjoy the lifestyle of a retired chief executive, a privilege he had earned but lost only through an unfortunate set of circumstances. This stolid warrior had made his last conquest because he and his parent board of directors had not conducted their due diligence to uncover the illegal practices. Neither had the acquired subsidiary company board (which Charlie also chaired) been close enough to a working partnership with its CEO to recognize the practice of classical price-fixing procedures.

Charlie had been surprised. While ignorance of the law or the internal practices of a new management group may be understandable, it is not pardonable. Charlie had learned the lesson Sir Roy Griffiths' colleagues at Sainsburys had practiced for close to 125 years: A board should never distance itself from its management.

The partnership that holds the powers of both the CEO and the board together is never at rest. Like any kind of close relationship, it requires work and constant adjustment and diligent attention to details. Two store visits a week, fifty-two weeks a year, may seem like an imposition. But it's simply smart business to keep in touch, especially if you don't want to be surprised.

REPRISE: ANCHORING POINTS FOR
SMART DIRECTORSHIP

Charles F. Kettering once commented that we should all be concerned about the future because we will have to spend the rest of our life there. Anchoring to a value system, a belief system, a point of view, or a future event is one good way to think heuristically about an uncertain future while we spend our life there.

Three of the heuristics (defined as exploratory, problem-solving techniques) employed in making judgment under uncertainty are representativeness (categorizing), scenarios, and anchoring. The phenomenon of anchoring involves a technique to estimate or imagine by starting from an initial value in the future that is adjusted to yield the final answer. Different starting points, or anchor values, yield different estimates that are biased toward the initial values.

A problem arises in the fact that one's value ranking changes as we grow more experienced, age, and enter later stages of life. What was a very attractive activity when we were in our thirties may not stir our interest when we are forty, sixty, or seventy. Anchor values change, the psychologists phrase it. The board, as a composite of individual directors, matures and develops under a program of smart directorship learning. Appendix B presents eighteen guidelines or characteristics for considering maturity and seven suggested criteria for further development of maturity and effectiveness.

This value change and maturation phenomenon is an argument for boardroom diversity of corporate directors in their background experience, age, and service considerations. The cardinal, anchor values of individuals may become incompatible as the complexity of an enterprise system increases.

Anchor values and their changes are the tap roots of covenantal relationships—person-to-person exchanges and connectivity. The nine anchoring points selected in this book for corporate boards of directors were chosen to help in two respects: (1) to provide significant footings for judgment and knowledge, and (2) to consciously platform the organizational learning process for directors toward obeying the unenforceable.

Appendixes

A

A Director's Do-It-Yourself Checkup: Are You Boardworthy for the 1990s?

LUSIVE STANDARDS and group anonymity have long masked individual directors' contribution to company performe. But with increasing public concern ut corporate behavior, critics are ask, "Are directors boardworthy?"

Until recently, it would have been incate, at best presumptive, to suggest t boards and their members should be bject to performance appraisals. But exsions from boardrooms, revelations of porate bribery, insider dealings, and er unacceptable practices, plus the inased frequency of restructuring and porate takeovers followed by lags in tain corporations' performance, have sed the issue of inadequate director effectiveness and performance. Codes of duct that some boards impose, or nect to impose, have not always matched er the social responsibility or responeness of companies or the expectations takeholders.

Some attempt to self-evaluate ardworthiness" thus seems warranted.

It emerges as a natural response to recent events and related issues that provoke several to-the-point questions: What is the role of a corporate director today? Why didn't the directors act? How much of board service is honorary? How much is substantive? Whom does the director represent first—the public, management, employees, or shareholders? What behavioral norms or codes, if any, steer individual directors, in addition to those set forth in legal doctrines and regulations?

Criteria for membership on corporate boards traditionally have been elusive and purposely ambiguous. Boardworthiness is often assumed to accompany election of a director. And too few boards, board chairmen, and chief executive officers ever really tackle the question of their effectiveness. Considering the aroused public concern over corporate behavior, the tolerance of shareholders and fellow directors to cases of dereliction of duty and pedestrian oversight in the boardroom remains surprisingly high.

his appendix expands on the article, "A Director's Performance Appraisal," by the author, which eared in *Directors and Boards*, 17 (3): 16–25, published by MLR Holdings, Inc., Philadelphia.

But changes in laws and government regulations plus mounting social, consumer, and employee pressures are dousing any lasting flicker of a directorship's honorary nature by demanding substantive performance and public accountability. No longer can a board be confined to an exclusive group selected by the CEO or chairman. No more can a director merely direct (if he or she ever did), or just merely reflect. Questions of whether the director is an advocate or an advisor, a tiger or a lamb, a figurehead or a keeper of a fiduciary trust, are welling up in boardrooms. We are witnessing an overdue rethinking of the philosophy, concept, structure, composition, role, and effectiveness of the board and the fitness of individual directors.

Some theorists believe that an aggregation of persons of like minds and philosophies with similar goals and values will ultimately emerge in a "proper" board. In practice, however, the result is often something else. The primary benchmarks of boardworthiness are imbedded, *inter alia*, in legal doctrines of fiduciary trust, standards of care, loyalty, due diligence, corporate opportunity, and conflict of interest.

Many behavioral and conduct issues thus remain to be clarified. Many board members spend up to 20-plus days a year preparing for and attending meetings. This poses the question of actual value added by a director.

Evaluative Criteria

In evaluating a board and an individual director's effectiveness, two basic questions must be answered: How well is the board of directors relating to current needs of the company? How well does the board deal with the futurity of current business decisions? There are also at least six categories of evaluative criteria that relate to the effectiveness of directors in meeting

present and future needs. Briefly, the criteria focus on:

1. *Commitment and interest of individual directors.* The time is past when the purpose of being on a board is to be a member of the "club". The director's potential liabilities are too great, and a deep interest and commitment to the role of director and to the company are a primary requirement.

2. *Capacity and competence of individual directors related to the needs of the corporation.* Boards need members with business and professional know-how pertinent to the corporation's activities. Such linkage is, of course, provided in part by inside directors. It is often important however, to have outside, independent directors available as a resource, individuals with experience or knowledge of the state of the art of technology, finance, politics, law, international affairs, communications, social and environmental problems, and other pertinent areas.

3. *Availability of directors for counsel and committee work.* To what extent directors should participate in functional or operational affairs of the corporation poses a nagging question. But many American and European organizations are engaging in interesting experiments, including some large companies that have as many as six or more standing committees through which directors do much of their work. These committee members have the problem of maintaining an evaluative posture in their board's role and not invading areas of executive responsibility.

4. *Directors' nonconflicting bridges and networks to allied sectors.* Any apparent or real conflict of interest between directors' responsibilities to the firm they serve as board members and to any other outside activity or organizations should be resolved. Normally, it is taboo to be connected with a supplier, major customer, or competitor. Even connections

th law firms, investment houses, accounting firms, or consultants raise the question of how independent a director can be on many issues before the board. Nonetheless, sensitivity to and linkages with the banking, educational, governmental, international, and military institutions and other key communities can be important attributes of board members.

5. *General functional strength of individual directors.* Boards need members with basic functional talents to provide imaginative policy guidance and aid in such major areas as general management, finance, law, strategic planning, facilities management, real estate, environmental health and safety assurance, social and political policy, and international affairs.

6. *A director's role as a change agent.* Boards can exercise the role of change agent for the enterprise. This role differs from the traditional judicial performance of making go or no-go decisions on management proposals. A board can develop ideas on its own. But this requires an atmosphere conducive to change and individual board members able and willing to suggest going beyond traditional evaluative or judicial processes. Imagination, innovation, and willingness to suggest trying new concepts and ideas are attributes vitally needed in many boardrooms.

It isn't easy to objectively self-examine our own effectiveness as a director and to determine whether we have the needed talent, wisdom, experience, inspiration, imagination, independence, and risk attitude. In addition, a director must have the ability to develop appropriate social contracts with fellow board members.

DO-IT-YOURSELF CHECKUP

w would you evaluate yourself? Here are some suggestions:

Competence as director

Honors Fits in well and with distinction. Personally competent. Effective presence. Experienced. Influential. Respected. Outstanding peer relationships in profession, business or community, and with other board members.

Rounds out board strengths, abilities, experience, and subjective judgement.

Good communicator.

Ideologically oriented toward socio-economic philosophy relevant to corporate welfare and conduct and supports them.

Understands the difference between governing and managing a corporate enterprise.

Is clear on the long-term economic mission of the enterprise and the delicate balance with social accountability.

Pass Meets most criteria above but may not be optimal when compared with talent available elsewhere.

Fail Talents largely duplicative of others, or less rounded out. While similar talents are often useful, director is substantially below level of compe-

tence and experience of others. Absence incurs no handicap to boa
functions. Realistically, must be discounted as having significant inp
to soundness of decisions or effectiveness of board. Does not fit nee
of corporation.

2. Applied ethics

Honors   High integrity.

Free of and sensitive to perceived or actual conflicts of interest.

Exemplary code of behavior, morals, beliefs, attitudes, and values.

Disciplined ethical thinking and approach to duties and obligations
cultures in which director and corporation find themselves.

Understands "servanthood without dominance" and "obedience to th
unenforceable" (or corporate manners).

Initiates discretionary digging into corporate affairs as far as ethics ar
conduct of directors, officers, and employees are concerned. Relate
such to industry, legal, cultural, political, moral environments.

Is sensitive to the "tone at the top" and ethical work climate of the ente
prise.

Comprehends the company's work climate, moral atmosphere, and "ju
community" considerations in the social context of the company's ar
director's moral and ethical behavior.

Understands that existence of an ethical work climate requires that no
mative systems in the organization be institutionalized.

Has at his or her command ethical considerations of policy, practice,
issues under review.

Has courage to appropriately pose ethical and moral questions. Apropo
one researcher commenting on the anguished ethics dilemma in a
plied ethics said, "You're simply out in no man's land." Scholars do th
theoretical and foundation work. Practitioners, such as corporate dire
tors, do the derivative work so that people in applied ethics situatior
"are in the inherently comic position of carrying water from wells the
haven't dug to fight fires they can't quite find."

Pass   Meets most criteria above. Not zealous on ethics. Soundly grounded c
moral principles. Adherence to ethical standards, norms, and values.

Does not cover up or experiment with questionable ethics.

Responds to investigative efforts where questions may be involved.

Is conscious of and sensitive to conflicts of interest perceived, actual
potential.

Fail   Is insensitive to many ethical and moral questions.

Is flexible on principles of conduct.

Directly or indirectly, covers up questionable practices. Lacks stron
sense of honesty and integrity generally attributed to those in position
of public trust.

3. Independence

Honors   Thinks, speaks, and acts independently, with confidence and courage.

Focuses on free-standing posture where independent decision is important.

Avoids real or apparent conflicts of interest.

Resists tendency of board toward a self-perpetuating protectorate unresponsive to change.

Is a free thinker.

Espouses a reasoned, independent directorate.

Does not behave independently for sake of being an iconoclast or a rev-
olutionary character. Is objective when considering trade-offs and consequences.

Is always willing to risk rapport and collateral with chairman, board members, and chief executive officer in taking a reasoned, independent position.

Understands and supports proper, albeit complex, relationships of the
board members with the chairman, the CEO, and executive management.

Would relinquish directorship rather than be considered captive.

Pass   Respected for independent role.

Not as prickly an independent as qualifications above.

Speaks up on critical matters requiring objective opinion.

Not captive of the chairman, chief executive officer, or other member of
the board, although may be influenced at times by their dispositions
toward matters.

Potential conflict areas—real or perceivable—are openly explored, and an
objective position is adopted.

Fail   Is a captive to members of board or outside parties.

Functions as surrogate for other interests.

Is primarily dependent on political currents.

Lacks will or courage to speak and act independently.

. Social and environmental consciousness

Honors   Appreciates impact of the company's activities on the social and ecological nature of the environment.

Is perceptive to the impact of external, social and environmental forces
on employees, customers, suppliers, and other stakeholders on the
company.

Understands the boundary of all forces affecting the achievement of the
purpose and mission of the organization.

Comprehends the "appreciative power field" of the enterprise consisting
of relevant economic, technological, political, military, social, environmental, health, and safety factors affecting company performance.
When actively "appreciating," the director is in a receptive mode, listening, understanding, valuing, and sharing the perceptions.

Explores these situations, advising the company where influence power
may be effected to help establish appropriate patterns of working relationships between the enterprise and social and environmental forces.

Recognizes and accepts the stewardship role of the board, maintaining

an open system for the enterprise and its multiple interfaces with
social and ecological environment.

Encourages the enterprise to refine its overall risk management postu
This insures adequate awareness, policy, functions, and auditing
governance and management processes for environmental, health a
safety assurance, crisis management, damage control programs, a
public and employee relations initiatives. This also includes suggest
parameters within which people can control themselves versus prov
ing specific goals. Examples: codes of conduct, social learning me
ods, social responsiveness, and social responsibility considerations

Views the corporation as both a work-sharing and risk-sharing entity
system.

Pass   Meets most criteria above.

Does not necessarily assume a leadership role regarding this sensiti
subjective attribute.

Is knowledgeable and supportive of those who champion reasoned c
sciousness-raising.

Is knowledgeable and sensitive about social and environmental c
cerns, activists' pressures, and the realities of adopting a progress
attitude in this regard.

Spends time evaluating the company's relevant policies and practices.

Takes part, when asked, in auditing the processes used to assure soc
and environmental accountability.

Fail   Is insensitive or apathetic to social and environmental issues. May be
flexibly counter-activist, counter-reform, or disinterested in corpor
conduct regarding these social and environmental issues and/or th
consequences.

May represent a single-minded proponent of corporate economic
countability with only token responsibility for social and environmen
impacts.

5. Preparedness as director

Honors   Briefs self thoroughly. Shows sincere interest.

Spends extra time with chairman and CEO on relevant issues.

Knows key officers and some back-up managers.

Visits facilities as appropriate.

Exchanges views with others in corporate world.

Respects confidentiality.

Knows corporation's history, philosophy, style, and strategic plans.

Keeps abreast of professional and international trends.

Understands statutory and fiduciary roles.

Stays current on legislative and regulatory matters.

Is a continuing student of corporate enterprise, governance, and m
agement.

Exercises responsibility to shape policy and insure continuing mana
ment.

Keeps out of executive-administrative zone.

Assists in corporate growth.

Understands director and officer liability insurance protection and indemnification measures taken by the corporation for his or her personal protection.

Pass   Is generally familiar with corporation's philosophy, opportunities, and problems. Needs limited self-education on the business and director function.

Is reasonably current with company and industry problems.

Understands power separation between directorate and executive management.

Fail   Little knowledge of, but some interest in, general state of company and industry.

Sporadic self-briefing.

Doesn't try very hard beyond attending meetings.

Contributes little thoughtful input.

Gets more from association than offers—in wisdom, reputation, advice, enthusiasm, and support.

6. Practice as director

Honors   Thoroughly prepared.

Does homework and understands reports and background materials.

Communicates privately and constructively with chairman or chief executive between meetings.

Avoids surprises.

Asks probing questions focused on policy and strategy rather than tactics and details.

Does not interrogate to show off knowledge.

Director work is mostly talk and thinking.

It is more symbol-intensive than labor-intensive.

Insists on and gets information necessary for decision making.

Does not invade province of executive management.

Conducts himself or herself so that corporation is satisfied with director's effectiveness.

Fulfills statutory and fiduciary requirements.

Keen ability to evaluate CEO, senior management, and company performance.

Participates on committees when asked.

Key resource to management and board.

Introduces new thinking.

Active in civic affairs and furthering education of directors.

Pass   Generally prepared on issues.

Fulfills statutory and fiduciary role.

Reasonably able in evaluative role.

Participates intelligently and constructively at meetings.

Exhibits prior thought, interest, and consideration rather than performs for peers' benefit, or to show that he or she is an interested director worth the fees.

Fail   Little evidence of study prior to meetings. Uses meeting time to develo
            background by asking questions dealt with in briefing papers.
            Causes some frustration because of amateur performance.
            Allows leadership to fall to others.
            Misses meetings too frequently without legitimate excuse.
            Discussion, if any, is often negative and unhelpful.
            Really is not with it.
            Cannot truly be considered committed, responsible, or interested.

7. Committee activity

Honors   Serves usefully on at least one important committee.
            Has ideas and enthusiasm.
            Uses abilities and influence constructively.
            Does homework.
            Understands process of committee work, particularly relations with exe
            utive management.

Pass   Nominally loyal to committee responsibilities.
            Attends meetings and carries out some duties with acceptable interest. I
            definitely subordinate to the committee chairman.
            Does little work on his or her own.
            Relies on committee staff work.
            Fair attendance.
            Little effort exerted outside of meetings.

Fail   Not particularly well prepared and misses sessions frequently.
            Uses committee time to think about assignment.
            Brings no new thinking.
            Often opposed to consensus without credible rationale.
            Little sense of responsibility toward committee, even avoids assignment:
            Operates passively without participative actions except attending som
            scheduled meetings.

8. Development process of the corporate enterprise

Honors   Owns (but does not trade in) responsible amount of corporate stock i
            relation to own resources.
            Makes penetrating suggestions on innovations, strategic directions, an
            planning.
            Knowledgeable about trends and externalities.
            Understands the impact of ownership on productivity in a closely he
            corporation.
            Recognizes shareowners as the only voluntary constituency whose rela
            tion with the corporation often does not come up for periodic renewa
            Consequently, sees that, in the development process, governanc
            mechanisms protect shareholder interests and enhances shareholde
            value.
            Questions officers in appropriate manner and at proper times on finar
            cial strategy.

Helps win support of outside organizations, customers, suppliers, and public investors.

Relates corporation to new business opportunities ethically through direct and indirect participation.

Positive force and independent thinker with interest in future directions and equity patterns of the corporation. Believes in conscious promotion of economic growth with social fairness.

Pass   Holds nominal amount of company stock.

Occasionally explores business issues with financial, commercial, or technical community on behalf of company when encouraged to do so.

Average interest in conventional growth prospects.

Not particularly identified as a strong supporter of forward innovative programs, but does not unduly resist them.

Fail   Does not participate, even nominally, in furthering financial, commercial, or technical connections with the organization, profession or industry. If required by law, holds token amount of shares, but purchase is not usually of own volition.

Brings nothing substantive to deliberations of company growth vectors or dimensions.

Has rearview-mirror mentality.

Resists change and does not keep up with future expectations and trends in the industry, business, or geographical theater of company activities.

. Ambassadorship

Honors   Enthusiastic, effective spokesperson with knowledge of the business and/or industry.

Suggests ways to use outside relationships on behalf of company.

Relates corporation to the outside world in credible ways.

Sophisticated in public relations process and possesses impressive presence.

Pass   Friendly, personable, and articulate.

Occasionally and carefully enhances relationships on behalf of corporation.

Mentions company constructively.

Responds when asked to represent company interests.

Fail   Apathetic attitude. Inactive ambassadorship.

Keeps low profile.

Little visible corporate connection.

. Attendance

Honors   Attends all meetings or has valid excuse for missing a meeting.

Shows interest and comes prepared.

Plans ahead and requests forward schedules.

Meetings are high on his or her appointment priority. Optimizes exposu
to others at meetings.
Makes special effort to be at stockholders' annual meeting.

Pass Attends most board and committee meetings or has valid excuse.
Understands importance of attendance.
Puts attendance first in scheduling other activities.

Fail Poor attendance.
Invalid or questionable excuses for missing either board or committe
meetings.
Provides nothing between times for the chief executive officer, board,
committee chairperson to think about.
Doesn't appear interested enough to regularly attend meetings.

11. Hierarchy of personal needs

Honors Note: Maslow's positive theory of human motivation applies to directo
ship service in three of five salient needs. The first two personal nee
(that is, physiological and safety needs) are satisfied before nominatio
and election to a board.
For a director to qualify for honors, the challenge and rewards of boa
service must be satisfying in all three of the higher needs: belongi
needs (sociability, acceptance); esteem needs (status, prestige, a
knowledgement); and the highest need, self-actualization (personal fu
fillment and growth).
Views directorship as an ethical service.
Service on the board is seen as an effective way society devised to balan
the ethic of competition with the ethic of service to the owners a
stakeholders of a corporate enterprise.
Strives to improve public trust and confidence in corporation and i
board members by exemplary personal conduct while fulfilling the ro
of a director, serving in a worthy, prestigious position.
Assists the corporation to achieve "vanguard" status regarding long-ter
perspective of distinguished corporate conduct. "Vanguard" compani
are those seeking to serve stakeholder interests rather than obsesse
with profits. Data show vanguard companies are more profitable in th
long run.
Enjoys the exhilaration and challenge in tackling vexatious issues as ste
ard of owners' and stakeholders' interests.
Receives gratification from the recognition from serving effectively on
competent board of a reputable, progressive firm.
By their approval or disapproval, boards direct the flow of capital, bo
financial and human.
Board decisions often start new businesses or industries and provi
gratification to those wielding board power.
Team player.
Extension and empowerment of directors' external networks can be be
eficial and psychically rewarding.
Receives personal fulfillment by taking part (with a select group of r

spected peers) in governing an enterprise in risky, uncertain circumstances.

Pass   Achieves a sense of belonging to the board of directors.

Attains social and professional acceptance from other members of the board.

May or may not enjoy the exhilaration of challenging issues. But is able to cope with the tension, complexity, and uncertainty inherent in certain boardroom decisions.

Is comfortable with team play requirements of effective board work.

Fail   Does not fulfill or experience belonging, esteem, or self-actualization needs from board service.

Has difficulty integrating with and relating to other directors. Does not enjoy or appreciate the ethic-of-service aspect.

Views directorship primarily in terms of prestige, director compensation, privileges, and emoluments.

12. Chairman of the board

Honors   Understands and believes in significant difference of roles of chairman (as agent of the board) and chief executive officer (appointed by and responsible to the board) whether both titles are held by one person or by separate persons.

Prepares carefully for meetings.

Gives thoughtful consideration to making meetings the most effective use of time of those assembled.

Insists on reports being properly prepared in advance

Distinguishes between material for information and material requiring board action.

Keeps discussions on major strategic or policy matters.

Insists on advance review of presentations where appropriate and when needed.

Is competent in chairing and managing group dynamics.

Thoughtful in agenda management.

Considers what executive officers need to focus on at meetings and coaches them on director education and perceptions.

Properly balances exposure of board to advocate and adversary views on major issues.

Encourages constructive debate and independent viewpoints.

Endeavors to make each meeting an interesting and rewarding experience for each participant.

Effective leader with personal respect and established collateral with each member.

Sees that candidates are developed for chairman and CEO succession, whether both titles are held by one or by separate persons.

This involves education and testing process plus understanding of different qualifications for chairmanship and chief executive officer roles.

Pass   Adequate moderator in sum (but not extensive interest or expertise in many considerations above).

Passive interest in facing issues or improving director motivation.
Not forceful leader.
Constructive attitude, but reactive mode.

Fail   As moderator, acts with little skill, enthusiasm, or insight.

Delegates most governance issues to chief executive officer, if the chairman is a non-executive.

Not strong advocate or does not understand (or believe in) explicit separation of roles (even when held by the same person) of chairman and chief executive officer for normal, stabilized corporate situations.

Does little to enable smooth, timely chairman or CEO succession.

Does not effectively encourage discussion.

Is nervous with conflict at meetings.

Wishy-washy attitude on critical issues.

Does not encourage members to contribute to top management in strategy or policy formation.

Does not exercise leadership in motivating directors.

13. Special service

If service of a certain director is of vital importance in a significant way to the corporation—even though the appraisal of boardworthiness in some other areas of directorship may be low—a special criterion often may be added in a flexible board situation. This special status may be justified and attributable, for example, to an expert professional role, a celebrity role, or a controlling shareowner's representative.

A situation may arise where regular attendance at meetings is geographically or otherwise difficult, but where a director's relationship makes possible distinguished service of a nature not easily achieved with another person. Former government, military, professional, academic, or business service of an outstanding nature are examples (as in the case of nationals remotely located from corporate headquarters) with special credentials in a cultural or geographical area where credibility and local acceptance are vital to functioning in the region. Criteria may override a deficit in one or more of the director's attributes. Lack of a passing rating in certain attributes may be waived because of such special service.

Self-Examination Guidelines

Under the self-examination guidelines suggested here, the rating of *Honors* signifies director service of distinction with overall high effectiveness. *Pass* implies the director is satisfactory on essentially all counts. *Fail* means the director is unacceptably deficient in contributions, performance, or effectiveness.

The do-it-yourself checkup is a suggested thought process. It is not meant to be constraining or overly quantitative.

Judgment as to which attributes are essential in order for a director to be effective will vary. This depends upon the philosophy, concept, and policies of the board; the value systems of individuals on the board; the nature of the corporate enterprise; and the environment in which the corporation operates. Certainly there should be limited quarrel with the vital need for a director to

it the board assignment in terms of qualifi-
ations and competence, integrity, ethics,
and ability to be an ambassador on behalf
of the corporation.

Director's Do-It-Yourself Checkup

Attribute Category	Honors	Pass	Fail	Special
1. Competence	_____	_____	_____	_____
2. Applied Ethics	_____	_____	_____	_____
3. Independence	_____	_____	_____	_____
4. Social and Environmental Consciousness	_____	_____	_____	_____
5. Preparedness	_____	_____	_____	_____
6. Practice	_____	_____	_____	_____
7. Committee Activity	_____	_____	_____	_____
8. Development	_____	_____	_____	_____
9. Ambassadorship	_____	_____	_____	_____
0. Attendance	_____	_____	_____	_____
1. Hierarchy of Personal Needs	_____	_____	_____	_____
2. Chairmanship	_____	_____	_____	_____
3. Special Service	_____	_____	_____	_____

egend: Par effectiveness embraces Categories 1 through 11. Chairmanship and Special Service categories
re examined separately. *Competence, Applied Ethics, Independence,* and *Social and Environmental Con-
ciousness* are considered essential attributes.

Distinctive effectiveness (above par)	At least four *Honors*, maximum one *Fail* (exclusive of 1, 2, 3, 4).
Acceptable effectiveness (par)	At least one *Honors*, maximum one *Fail* (exclusive of 1, 2, 3, 4).
Fair to poor effectiveness (below par)	No *Honors*, several *Fails* (including one or more of 1, 2, 3 or 4).

Obviously, self-evaluations need to consider the enterprise culture, the evolutionary stage of the enter-
rise, the ownership pattern, and the environment in which the company exists. No two enterprises or
oards are alike and therefore I can see no way to standardize these categories.

This framework is offered only to start you thinking about the importance of personal effectiveness in
he boardroom.

B

Board Maturity and Development

We tend to view boardroom ways and means most often in monetary terms: earnings per share, dollars invested per employee, and a host of financial ratios. But such monetary measures are relatively useless in gauging a board as immature or mature. Proxy statements, disclosure documents, SEC forms 10K, 10Q, 8K, annual reports, comfort letters, and other corporate forms of communications are heavily oriented toward numbers. Comments on corporate conduct or individual contributions by directors are limited in most instances. The following guidelines are suggested as items reflecting the maturity of a directorate.

A board may be considered mature when it has satisfied the legal requirements and when directors are involved with regard to the following:

1. Basic statutory and fiduciary compliance, including performance of principal duties for the corporation served. These are duty of loyalty, duty of care, and duty of attention and preparedness.

2. An established code of ethics for the corporation.

3. Appropriate degree of independent, disinterested members of the board to ensure objective check and balance on corporate decisions, particularly in audit compensation, director nomination (and criteria), indemnification provisions, and management succession matters.

4. The board's existential nature, including clear corporate vision, objectives, and strategic plans.

5. Recognition of responsibilities and responsiveness to society, which sanctions the existence of the corporation.

6. Understanding the environmental health and safety hazards and obligations inherent in the type of business the company chooses to engage in and the taking of appropriate and responsible safeguard actions.

7. Establishment of board processes and organization to monitor corporate conduct and integrity of the corporation's systems.

8. Delegation and retention of powers, responsibility, and authority necessary to conduct the affairs of the company effectively.

9. Explicit policy and procedures for evaluating corporate board and management performance.

10. Adequate and reliable information system to keep directors informed on company matters. Directors have a responsibility to maintain a current understanding of developments in the industry, the securities laws, and the obligations and liabilities of directors.

11. An effective, constructive, mutually trustful interface between the board, the chairman, and the executive management, particularly the CEO if separate from the chairman.

12. Programmed replacement of directors lost by retirement or otherwise, with a confidential woodbox of potential candidates who have been screened and investigated regarding their qualifications to ensure that they represent the experience and wisdom needed by the board.

13. Separate roles and incumbents for the chairman, as an agent of the board, and the CEO. Exceptions to this pattern of separate incumbency are often sound and important but are company specific.

14. Where appropriate, stock ownership by the individual directors (at least nominal and not dominating).

15. Faithful attendance by directors at board and committee meetings and devotion of a responsible amount of time to directorship.

16. Positive directors' contributions in the form of corporate ambassadorial roles in the community and marketplace.

17. Stimulating, trustful, and respectful peer relationships within the board.

18. Disaster and emergency plans formulated by management of the corporation for handling the consequences of such a major interruption.

Given a good rating on these eighteen characteristics of a mature board (there are undoubtedly a few more), there can be further growth in an economic, social, or cultural sense. For example, the board can improve its flexibility, its initiative, its resources, and its roles. This further development of maturity and effectiveness of the board may be in terms of the following:

- Improvement in quality of decision making.
- Strengthening of the rapport of the directors with each other and within executive ranks.
- Enhancement of corporate climate for executive recognition and development by increased exposure of the directors to personnel, plant sites, offices, and laboratories.
- Extension of the perceived boundaries of director concern for environmental, social, technological, and political domains that surround or can impact the corporation.
- Increased but carefully controlled participation by directors on board committees and as expert resource persons when qualified and requested by the chairman.
- A change agent or a catalyst introducing new concepts, new directions, new objectives, and a constant reexamination of the long-term viability and integrity of the business in which the corporation is engaged. When new thinking is introduced for the company to explore, the board should be able to stimulate management. This change-agent role becomes imperative when called upon in crisis situations or when management fails to carry out its proper functions.
- Upgrading of the talent and resources of the board by adding distinguished individuals to the membership, subject to shareholder approval, for the purpose of broadening the resources on the board.

The latent capacity of most boards to improve is tremendous, and many companies have made great strides to tap such unutilized capacity for improved corporate governance. Spreading this movement to a particular directorate requires raising the consciousness of the potential and requires emotional acceptance of the merit of maturing or fully developing the board. It also requires enlightened leadership of the board, most properly the chairman's role. It may also come from other effective or psychological leaders among the board members. The priority of concerns of a board varies considerably with its state of maturity and the nature of the institution being served.

Nonprofit institutions, by their very nature, place social and noneconomic objectives ahead of profitability and return on investment measures of a business corporation. This different emphasis does not diminish the social responsibilities of shareowners and directors of a profit-making enterprise but it defines certain boundaries of social responsibility for the profit-oriented corporation.

Notes

PREFACE

1. Amos Tversky and Daniel Kaheman, "Judgement Under Uncertainty: Heuristics and Biases," *Science* 185 (1974): 1124–1132.

2. American Management Association, "Report on International Management: East–West Management in the New Europe," research report, AMA, New York, 1993.

3. Dirk R. Dreux IV, "Financing Family Business: Alternatives to Selling Out or Going Public," *Family Business Review* 3, no. 3 (1990): 225–243.

MOULTON'S MANNERS

1. William Hazlitt, "Spirit of the Age, or Contemporary Portraits," *The Examiner* (1825).

CAVEAT LECTOR (AND WOULD-BE DIRECTOR)

1. Robert K. Mueller, *Behind The Boardroom Door: The Ultimate Arena of Corporate Power* (New York: Crown Publishers, 1984).

1 GROUPTHINK PATHOLOGY: HOW TO AVOID THIS

1. American Management Association, "Building a Power Partnership: CEOs and Their Boards of Directors," The Presidents Association, Special Report, New York, 1993.

2. Robert K. Mueller, "Directors Don't Have To Be Perfect," *Directors & Boards* 18, no. 3 (1994): 10.

2   LIMITATIONS TO LIVE WITH:
DIRECTORS DON'T HAVE TO BE PERFECT

1. American Management Association, "Boardworthiness: From a President's and Director's Perspective," The Presidents Association, Special Report, The Chief Executive Officers' Division of the AMA, New York, 1992.

2. The observations are drawn from Robert K. Mueller, *Behind The Boardroom Door: The Ultimate Arena of Corporate Power* (New York: Crown Publishers, 1984).

3   THE OYSTER NOT THE SHELL:
ENTERPRISE VERSUS CORPORATION

1. Bayless Manning, "Governing the Large Incorporated Enterprise: How to Get It Wrong." Presentation at the World Management Congress, New York, September 21, 1989, 1–2.

2. American Management Association, "Report on International Management: East–West Management in the New Europe," research report, AMA, New York, 1993.

3. Stephen Nesbitt, "Long-term Records from Corporate Governance," Wilshire Associates, November, 1993.

4   THE COVENANTAL DIVIDE:
CONTRACTUAL VERSUS COVENANTAL RELATIONSHIPS

1. Douglass C. North, *Institutions, Institutional Change and Economic Performance* (New York: Press Syndicate of the University of Cambridge, 1990).

2. Robert Axelrod, "An Evolutionary Approach to Norms," *American Political Science Review* 80 (1984): 1095–III.

3. North, *Institutions*, 42.

4. W. Richard Scott, "The Adolescence of Institutional Theory," *Administrative Science Quarterly* 32 (1987): 493–511.

5. Aleksandr Isayevich Solzhenitsyn, *A World Split Apart*, Commencement address delivered at Harvard University, June 8, 1978, translated by Irina Ilovayskaya Alberti (New York: Harper & Row, 1978).

6. Edward Gross and Gregory O. Stone, "Embarrassment and the Analysis of Role Requirements." In *People in Places: The Sociology of the Familiar*, edited by Arnold Birenbaum and Edward Saragin (New York: Praeger, 1973).

7. Max Depree, *Leadership is an Art* (New York: Dell Publishing, 1989).

8. American Management Association, "Building a Power Partnership: CEOs and Their Boards of Directors," The Presidents Association, Special Report, New York, 1993.

9. Charles Handy, *The Age of Unreason* (Boston, Mass.: Harvard Business School Press, 1990). A forward-looking dissertation of tomorrow's organizations in an era of wrenching, disjunctive change that will require new thinking from corporate leaders.

5 POWER IN PINSTRIPES:
PARTNERSHIP OF CEO AND THE BOARD

1. Sidney Finkelstein, "Power in Top Management Teams: Dimensions, Measurement and Validation," *Academy of Management Journal* 35, no. 3 (1992): 505–538.

2. James L. Fisher, "How Presidents Can Wield Power," *Association of Governing Boards (AGB) Reports* (September/October, 1988): 20–24.

3. Peter A. French, "Publicity and the Control of Corporate Conduct: Hecter Prynne's New Image." In *Ethics and Social Concern*, edited by Anthony Serafini (New York: Paragon House, 1989). First published as Chapter 14 of *Corporate and Collective Responsibility* (New York: Columbia University Press, 1984). See these references for fifty-six pages of thoughtful research and study on the social stigmatization theory.

4. J. Angelo Corlett, "French on Corporate Punishment: Some Problems." In *Ethics and Social Concern*, edited by Anthony Serafini (New York: Paragon House, 1989): 363–373.

5. Reprinted with permission of "Briefings from the Editors," *Harvard Business Review* by Steven E. Prokesch (September–October, 1993): 10. Copyright 1993 by the President and Fellows of Harvard College; all rights reserved.

6 NO BUSINESS LIKE CLOSELY HELD BUSINESS:
THE LARGER PARALLEL ECONOMY

1. An abbreviated version of this disguised case is included in Robert K. Mueller, *The Director's and Officer's Guide to Advisory Boards* (Westport, Conn.: Quorum, 1990). Quorum Books is an imprint of Greenwood Publishing Group, Inc., Westport, Conn.

7 TROUSERS OF DECORUM:
COVER-YOUR-BACKSIDE ETHICS

1. Clarence C. Walton, *The Moral Manager* (Cambridge, Mass.: Ballinger Publishing, 1988). This is one of the most important books on ethics that appeals to action-oriented leaders.

2. Verne E. Henderson, *What's Ethical In Business?* (New York: McGraw Hill, 1992).

8 A DIRECTOR'S GUIDE TO STAYING CLEAN:
SPIRIT AS WELL AS LETTER OF THE LAW

1. Emile Durkheim, *The Elementary Forms of the Religious Life* (Glenco, Ill.: Free Press, 1912).

2. John Fiske, *Elbert Hubbard's Scrap Book* (New York: Wm. H. Wise & Co., 1923).

3. Updated from Robert K. Mueller, *Behind The Boardroom Door: The Ultimate Arena of Corporate Power* (New York: Crown Publishers, 1984).

4. Robert K. Mueller, "The Joys of Directorship," *Directors and Boards* 11, no. 1 (1986): 7–10.

9   SMART DIRECTORSHIP: KNOWLEDGE AND JUDGMENT

1. C. Roland Christensen, David A. Garvin, and Ann Sweet, *Education for Judgement: The Artistry of Discussion Leadership* (Boston, Mass.: Harvard Business School Press, 1991).

2. John Dewey, *How We Think* (Lexington, Mass.: D. C. Heath, 1933).

3. L. L. Cummings, George P. Huber, and Eugene Arendt, "Effects of Size and Spacial Arrangements of Group Decision-Making," *Academy of Management Journal* VIII, no. 3 (1974): 460–475.

4. American Management Association, "Boardworthiness: From a President's and Director's Perspective," The Presidents Association, Special Report, The Chief Executive Officers' Division of the AMA, New York, 1992.

5. American Management Association, "Building a Power Partnership: CEOs and Their Boards of Directors," The Presidents Association, Special Report, New York, 1993.

Index

Moulton's Manners (*continued*) 114

Nepotism, 90–91
Networking, 119–120
NIFI (Nose In, Fingers In) model, 48
NIFO (Nose In, Fingers Out) model, 48
NOFO (Nose Out, Fingers Out) model, 48–49
North, Douglass C., 36

Obedience to the unenforceable, 28, 29, 37, 38, 102, 114
Organizational balance of power, 61, 62, 63, 65, 66, 67
Oyster-shell models, 28, 29, 30, 32

Peer evaluation, 22, 23
  attributes used in, 24, 25
  methods of, 24, 25
Peer power, 21, 22, 23, 24
Pepper v *Litton*, 110
Perks of directorship, 120
Portfolio partnership, 55
Power
  forms of, 71–72
  measurement of, 71
  types of, 69–70, 71
Profitability, 132
Publicly owned businesses, 46–47

Quality and quantity, in businesses, 132, 133, 134

Risk, 123

Sacred–profane theory, 107–108
Securities and Exchange Commission (SEC), 59
Self-sufficient partnership, 55
Shame, corporate, 72–73
Shareholders, power of, 69
Shawinigan Resins Corporation, 35–36, 51–54
Social contract model, 29, 32
Social organization, forms of, 84
Spatial arrangement, 125
  effect on boardroom situations, 125, 126, 127
Steinzor Effect, 125, 126
Strategic propriety, 37, 38
Strategies for Change: Logical Incrementalism, 19

Topside changes, 5, 7, 8
Transfer-of-power problems, 3, 4

Working Group on Corporate Governance, 5
World Bank, 30

Young President's Organization (YPO), 3, 4

ABOUT THE AUTHOR

ROBERT K. MUELLER is a director of Arthur D. Little, Ltd. (U.K.). Formerly chairman of the parent company, he served on its board for more than ten years. Prior to joining Arthur D. Little, Inc., in 1968, he was a director, member of the executive committee, and Vice President of Monsanto Company. He was also Chairman and President of Shawinigan Resins Corporation.

He has served as a director of Massachusetts Mutual Life Insurance Co., BayBanks, Inc., Mass Mutual Income Investors, Inc., and HEC Energy Corporation and as a trustee of the American–Austrian Foundation.

He currently is a director of Decision Resources Inc., Interneuron Pharmaceuticals Inc., and the National Association of Corporate Directors, as well as a trustee of The Business Ethics Foundation, The Cheswick Center, and the National Plastics Center and Museum. He is a Fellow of the International Academy of Management, the Institute of Directors (London), the New York Academy of Sciences, and the American Association for the Advancement of Science. He is also a Life Member of the American Management Association and a member of the AMA International Council, the Advisory Board of the Center for Business Ethics at Bentley College, and the Advisory Council of Energía Global, Inc.

A well-known speaker in professional circles, Mr. Mueller is the author of seventeen books on management and corporate governance matters, as well as numerous articles in scientific and business journals. Mr. Mueller served as chairman of the faculty for a Management of Technology session at the Salzburg Seminars in American Studies and subsequently served on that organization's board of directors and executive committee.

He received a B.S. degree in chemical engineering from Washington University and an M.S. degree in chemistry from the University of Michigan and has completed the Advanced Management Program at Harvard.